HAPPY GO→ LOCAL

The Smart Mom's Guide to Living the Good
(and Sustainable) Life!

LINSLY DONNELLY

Aadamsmedia
Avon, Massachusetts

Published by
Adams Media, a division of F+W Media, Inc.
57 Littlefield Street, Avon, MA 02322. U.S.A.
www.adamsmedia.com

ISBN 10: 1-4405-0008-8
ISBN 13: 978-1-4405-0008-4

Printed in the United States of America.

10   9   8   7   6   5   4   3   2   1

Library of Congress Cataloging-in-Publication Data
is available from the publisher.

This publication is designed to provide accurate and authoritative information with regard
to the subject matter covered. It is sold with the understanding that the publisher is not
engaged in rendering legal, accounting, or other professional advice. If legal advice or
other expert assistance is required, the services of a competent professional person should
be sought.

—From a *Declaration of Principles* jointly adopted by a Committee of the
American Bar Association and a Committee of Publishers and Associations

Many of the designations used by manufacturers and sellers to distinguish their product
are claimed as trademarks. Where those designations appear in this book and Adams
Media was aware of a trademark claim, the designations have been printed with initial
capital letters.

This book is available at quantity discounts for bulk purchases.
For information, please call 1-800-289-0963.

The Sustainable Forestry Initiative® program
promotes responsible environmental behavior
and sound forest management.

To our children, Cole and Tess.
You are the reason for tomorrow,
And the catalyst to play,
Today.

CONTENTS

ACKNOWLEDGMENTS

This page is the most fun to write. Thank you for the indulgence of reading it.

Happy-Go-Local made it into your hands thanks to your interest in making the world a better place. Also, my heartfelt thanks for:

- The love, inspiration, and raw cheerleading sung daily to me by the original Happy-Go-Local Mom, my mom, Ann Fisher Hunt. She is simply The Best. Thank you for seeing all things good in the world and in me.
- The living example of making a creative life work, and the one who got all the talent in the family, my brother, Wide Studio's very own Andrew Fisher Hunt.
- The shining example of quality, eco-friendly, *and* economy—well-packed with a grin—who is my mother-in-law, Mary Ellen Donnelly. And the creative thinker, rational planner, and sparkling storyteller who is my father-in-law, Thomas F. Donnelly.
- The yee-haw-hurrahs, soul-dance-glee, and oh-yes-you-cans woven across years and time zones from those known as The Girls—Didi "Shines" Engel, Crista Gordon Bailey, Sweet Stephanie Bowers, Lisa Kochie Ott, Ann-Marie Helling, Jan Swartz, Julie "Junk" Duryea, Jocelyn "Pants" Mangan, Eleanor "Cup" Carnes, Coco Lovely Jones, Leisle "Point Break" Bartley, Leslie "Smiles" Langford, Jill "Jalepeno" John, Brook BT Kremer,

Sums Starling, Schuyler Sly Rideout, Jean Bean Warren, Maria Mia Lile, and Kelly Belle Coberson.

- The ones who taught me how to dance on paper—The Writers' Group: Critita, Steph, E, and Joc as well as The Poet Jules.
- The enthusiasm, patience, and interest to read (and gently correct) early book iterations of Eagle Eye Liz Overson.
- The avid expert volunteering to first pressure test all assertions, Tom Donnelly.
- The faith of an avid risk taker and kindness of a fellow author who is most graciously my agent, Maryann Karinch.
- The generous champion, powerful word weaver, patient coach, and marvelous gift of an editor, Meredith O'Hayre. This book most certainly would never have been without her.
- The creative energy and graphic delights, compliments of Colleen Cunningham and Frank Rivera, as well as the fine-tooth combing patiently tuned by Kate Petrella.
- The daily joy and purpose for local roots alongside healthy longevity, our children, Cole and Tess.
- And, the unwavering hero who is my husband—Chris—the instigator . . . and that made all the difference.

INTRODUCTION

> "If you think you're too small to have an impact,
> try going to bed with a mosquito in the room."
> —Anita Roddick

As is true of most new babies, my son's birth brought a world of change. Playdates replaced double dates. Sleepless nights became the norm instead of a work project or big celebration event. My husband and I gave up hot-spot hopping for Netflix expertise. And, my perspective shifted from "It's Mostly about Me" to "It's All about Him."

As I saw life through my son's eyes, the world began to shrink from wherever my globetrotting friends and family had landed to only where we would be raising our family. The cacophony of "local living" and "sustainability" messages hit a newfound personal chord. A hypersensitivity to neighborly awareness replaced our jet-setter sense of global anonymity.

Now two children into the family game, I've realized that regardless of where we've traveled or where we may one day venture, where we live *right now* is the place where my family is going to be raised. If I want to impact our children's quality of life, I'd better get intimate with what is working and what isn't in our own backyard. If we like what is working, it is up to us to support it—financially or otherwise—to ensure it continues. And if it isn't working? Well—you can guess who needs to get involved and change it, yes?

"Going local" or "being sustainable" is about more than saving our planet. Yes, consuming goods produced closer to your home reduces the pollution released due to mass manufacturing and polluting tire treads. True, choosing organic products refuels your body and the earth much, much better than does buying overly engineered shampoos, tomatoes, and T-shirts. However, shifting your mindset to engage in your local community is about so much more than greenhouse gases and clean living (and, by the way, those things are pretty darn big). Going local is about—in a very real, day-to-day, smile at the person you pass on the street kind of way—saving ourselves.

We live in a world where we text message across the country while sitting with our family at dinner; where we know hundreds of virtual "friends" but can't name our next-door neighbors; where we buy closets full of clothes manufactured in towns we can't pronounce, but we couldn't pick our dry cleaner out of a lineup; and where we fervently debate foreign policy, but haven't met (or can't even identify) one city council person.

Going local and thinking sustainably require us to recalibrate the scale away from casual global citizenship to committed local residency. As you pay more attention to where your daily goods originate, how your neighbors live, and what businesses fuel your local economy, you can't help but engage in how to make your own backyard a better place. And, by caring more about our own backyards, collectively, we build a better assortment of them to patchwork together as "our world."

Transferring your family focus to living with more of a local, sustainable approach touches everything from becoming more eco-friendly and value conscious to gearing down your family's pace and amping up your do-it-yourself mentality. You'll begin to pay attention to who and what makes up your community—perhaps even starting with how you define your community. You may find you "get personal" for the first time and learn your grocer's name, map local farmers' markets, and meet the school board. You may aggressively pare down and buy less in order to soften your impact on your local environment. Or, you may just find that your family decides to simplify life in order to free up time for exploring your neck of the world's woods.

> ### → Mom to Mom: ←
> ### Field Trip to the Landfill
>
> Speaking of backyards, as you bring your family into your quest to stay local and reduce consumption, a field trip to your neighborhood landfill can be a powerful motivator. It's one thing to hear that the tallest thing—natural or manmade—in North America is a landfill. It's quite another to stand amidst your local trash and understand the endless toxicity we create every day. On our visit, I was amazed at how much beautiful, wide open space surrounded the landfill. Still, it looked as if the landfill area was getting tightly packed. When I asked about the seemingly "full" landfill, our guide shrugged his shoulders and said not to worry. He pointed to the vast, oceanside space and identified that as the next area for the site's "growth plan." What a heart-wrenching way to put our neighborhood green space to use.
>
> You may want to follow up the landfill tour with a trip to your local recycling center. The speed, efficiency, and grace with which these facilities and people work to resuscitate our throwaways into new materials inspires even the youngest in families to separate trash. Go to *www.therecyclingcenter.info* to find your local recycling center and set up a tour. You can also find your local landfill through your trash pickup service or in the yellow pages.

As our world grows more crowded, complicated and polluted each day, it seems the question is not, "Should we go local or get sustainable?" but "How do we put a viable, family-friendly plan in place?"

Happy-Go-Local will not make the scientific case for why you should want to shop within a 15-mile radius, nor will it argue the efficacy of local living reducing global warming (Al Gore is so much more compelling). Instead, *Happy-Go-Local* offers a how-to guide for the mom full of intention, but pressed for time. The handbook answers "how to go local" in the context of an already too busy day-to-day life. Flip through the guide to find tips organized around routine tasks such as:

- How to buy food
- What cosmetics to use and what clothes to wear
- How to work out
- How to invest to build your local economy
- How to celebrate holidays

Each section sorts recommendations based on level of ease and eco-impact. I've road-tested all products and confirmed recommended sources at time of printing.

Staying local or being sustainable does not mean being perfect or being deprived. It means opting for a better way to go about our daily lives. As you peruse tips, remember: *trying just one or two is enough to make a change.* Sift through what's here and decide what's realistic in your lifestyle. You'll likely surprise yourself by how much you can do with relatively little impact on your routine or budget. If you're inspired to learn more, go straight to the appendix for resources that help sort through the fact and fiction of being a better local citizen.

Last, keep in mind that I am not a scientist. There are plenty of people smarter than I who can explain the science, technology, regulations, and statistics behind many of the tips and recommendations (again, flip straight to the appendix for a complete resource list). I am a Mom and a well-meaning consumer. Overwhelmed by the avalanche of localvore articles and sometimes conflicting advice, I've sifted through recommendations to map them against daily activities. The outline and suggestions here result from a hectic Mom trying small steps in the hope there will be a thriving and pleasant community—local and global—for her children and grandchildren to enjoy. I hope the tips here make digging in to the backyard easier for you too.

> → **Mom to Mom:** ←
> ## Bringing the Whole Home Along with You
>
> It's tough to move the house ahead on a local path without buy-in from both Mom and Dad. Often the bank account offers the fastest path to convert a lukewarm advocate into a rabid zealot. Many actions that are good for our communities are even better for our wallets. Saving power, saving water, and saving gas all help save money, and many "sustainable" products come in value-oriented flavors. Look for the value sign tag (🏷) on cost-saving tips and recommendations throughout the book.

How to Use Your *Happy-Go-Local* Guide

Spend time on Chapters 1 and 2 to overview global themes such as recycling and understanding why your family's carbon footprint matters. In those chapters you'll also find a summary of all guidelines and tips, which you can then translate into daily actions by reading the more detailed chapters, 3 through 14. Each of these chapters categorizes tips and information by day-to-day activities such as choosing food and drink, caring for pets, and celebrating holidays, and then sorts them by effort and effectiveness. Read and digest what you can. Rip out the sections that help you the most, pass along others to friends, and then compost (see page 16 for the easiest, least messy ways to compost) what remains of the book.

At the start of each chapter, you'll see tools to help you focus on tips most relevant to your life routine and relative local living interest. Look for the Sustainability Screen and start with the tips in Box One. These are the easiest to do and deliver the highest impact. Move to Box Two (still easy, but slightly less impact) to add in a few more easy tips, realizing if we all took baby steps, we'd make great leaps. Box Three (high impact, but a bit more challenging to do) highlights the tougher tips worth reaching for; implementing one or two of these makes a big difference. In a perfect world, we'd do everything. But, in reality, some tips may get put on hold. You'll find those suggestions, which are tough to do and have lower impact, in Box Four.

Example Sustainability Screen

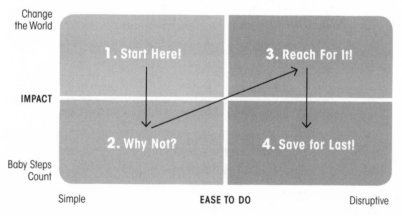

Scan beneath the Sustainability Screen for Eye Openers. These statistics offer motivation you can share at the dinner table, explaining why it's worth your family's time and energy to revise a particular chapter's area of your family's life.

Next, you'll see Local Life Guidelines. If you just want the cheat sheet for each chapter, start here with the laundry list of your local and sustainable to-do's. Tackle an area each week (or even one per month), and post the Local Life Guidelines on the refrigerator to corral everyone down the week's sustainability path.

If you want more detail on the why and how behind each of the Local Life Guidelines, go to the last section, The Nitty Gritty, which gives more in-depth explanation for each Guideline as well as the backstory on many of the tips and product recommendations.

To make life easier for the uber-busy woman in all of us, start with the first chapter, Happy-Go-Local: The Abbreviated Version. There you'll find the Top Ten Local Lifelines. Then skip to page 5 for Your Happy-Go-Local Plan. Use the checklist there to see what you'd like to implement, and flip to the chapter detail as needed. Your complete organization and resource list are in the back of the book in a section you can rip out and keep in your bag.

EYE OPENERS
We consume a lot of stuff:
- Homes throughout the world contain an average of 127 items; homes in the United States have more than 10,000.
- U.S. homes use twice the water as homes in other *developed* nations.
- America's average per-person CO_2 emission is five times the worldwide average.

- We generate 1,600 pounds of trash per person per year.
- Shifting just 1 percent of spending to purchasing local food products could increase local farmers' income by as much as 5 percent.

> "We must not, in trying to think about how we can make a big difference, ignore the small daily differences we can make which, over time, add up to big differences that we often cannot foresee."
>
> —Marian Wright Edelman

HAPPY-GO-LOCAL:
THE ABBREVIATED VERSION

> "Because we don't think about future generations,
> they will never forget us."
> —Henrik Tikkanen

With so many tips, changes, and products to evaluate, how do you know where to start? As you embark on your family's long-live-the-earth journey, focus on the Top Ten Local Life Lifelines. These guidelines act as signposts to help clarify where to get the biggest sustainability impact for your efforts.

1. Get to know your local scene.
Set up a "local" radius definition and get acquainted with stores, business, causes, and people close to home.

2. All politics are local.
Begin to dig in, learn the issues, the names and faces—and then, per-haps, make the leap to lead.

3. Set family targets.
Know and atone for your family's carbon footprint. First set a macro family baseline; see page 104 for options. Next do a sustainability

audit of your family's lifestyle and home to set micro family targets. Start at *www.lowimpactliving.com/projects/graph.*

4. Live the mantra: Buy none, buy less, buy used, buy local.

Warning: Digesting *Happy-Go-Local* may inspire an urge to revamp your home, work, and play gear. Resist the temptation. The most sustainable strategy you can put into place is to buy less. Buying less is a bonus for your home finances and the first step in your efforts. Think of these tips as your best replacement options, perhaps years down the line. If you start each day with the thought "I will buy less," you'll *build a more sustainable lifestyle—and bank account.* See Chapter 11 for tips on how to transfer that thinking to your children as well.

Try motivating older kids to spend less by adding a 10 percent "savings credit" to allowances. Since the number one thing you can do to be more sustainable is to bypass purchases, ask kids to present their case for purchases they skipped. You decide whether or not to "certify" them, and reward valid ones with an allowance bonus of 10 percent of the items' purchase price. See page 27 for other ideas for chores and allowance plans to motivate living with a long-term view.

5. Start from your backyard and buy from there.

Staying close to home enables you to know the source of your goods and invest in your community growth. Buy local, organic, or don't buy at all. When it comes to things you put in and on yourself, local, sustainable, organic goods take *much* better care of you and Mama Earth. Flip to Chapters 3, 4, and 5 for product recommendations and certification.

6. Recycle, and reinforce recycling.

When you buy recycled and reused goods, you keep things closer to home and build a bigger market for those goods. A bigger market means better products and pricing. Flip to page 14 for a summary of recycling how-to's, or check out *www.zerowaste.org* for tips. Recycled materials now show up in everything from cars and office supplies to clothes and home décor. Try *www.ciwmb.ca.gov/rcp*, *www.ecomall.com*, or *www.recycledproducts.com* to find items made from recycled materials.

7. Save your local resources.

Start with water: Take shorter showers; reduce faucet water pressure; install WaterSense appliances; cut the amount of water used in your toilet by placing bricks or filled milk gallon jugs in the tank; use shorter cycles on the dishwasher and washing machine. Find details in Chapter 6. Next, save power and shift to local sources (wind and solar!). Remember the basics: use less by turning off more. Consider Energy Star appliances, and swap your light bulbs for CFLs (compact fluorescent lights). Remember: in terms of pollution, one CFL bulb in your home = 1 million cars off the road. Use at-the-source power strips; tune up your heating and air conditioning systems; use more cold water than hot. Also consider an in-home energy audit—see page 104 for details.

8. Shed packaging.

First, choose products with no packaging whenever possible. Then choose materials made from more sustainable processes. Opt first for glass, then paper, and last—if at all—plastic. Try refillable pumps and compacts. Buy bigger sizes to spread the package impact across more of the product part.

9. Get really local and fuel-efficient.

Staying local translates into driving less—or not at all. When possible, tighten up your daily errands, activities, and events to a five- or even three-mile radius. When you do get behind the wheel, drive more efficiently. Amp up carpool efficiency. Motivate yourself to walk and bike just a few errands a week. Avoid the drive-through and try some method of your town's public transportation. (Don't like it? Change it. See Chapter 7 for ideas.) Drive a well-maintained car at lower speeds with less stops and starts. Consider alternate energy vehicles when it's time for the next purchase, or higher MPG models of wheels powered by fossil fuels. Big impact? Stay home a bit more often—drop one or more plane trips a year. See Chapter 7 for specific how-to's with kids' carriers, family activities gear, and carpool logistics.

10. Slowwwww down.

Downshift, dig in, and savor the path. Rework your mindset away from multitasking and uber-efficiency to relishing the ordinary and bothering to sweat the small—local—stuff. Carve out time to volunteer for local causes. Pause to notice the change in seasons with your children as you walk from to-do to to-do. Release the constant state of anxiety created by checking e-mail, texts, and voice mails. Delight in talking to your neighbors—and inhaling the local life surrounding you.

As you pick up tips and add product recommendations, share your expertise with your Mom network. Send on nuggets to your book club, Mommy & Me class, and family networks to help make everyone's sustainable journey a bit easier to put in place.

YOUR HAPPY-GO-LOCAL PLAN
FAMILY CHECKLIST

Chapters 1 & 2
Your Current State of Local Life, pages 1 and 11

- ◯ Hit "pause" and slow down
- ◯ Do a family and home energy audit
- ◯ Know your carbon footprint
- ◯ Revise your home recycling process
- ◯ Assign everyone in the house an area to oversee (including the car, garage, and yard)
- ◯ Do quarterly home sweeps to collect special-handling recyclables, donations, and hazardous waste disposal

Chapter 3
Keeping Your Family's Food and Drink Local, Sustainable, and Healthy, page 32

- ◯ Define "Our Local"
- ◯ Build the local food sources: CSAs, farmers' markets, co-ops, local grocers
- ◯ Increase our share of local, organic, and fair trade goods
- ◯ Sign up for a CSA share
- ◯ "Adopt" a farmer
- ◯ Start or join a dinner co-op
- ◯ Experiment with a patch of homegrown produce
- ◯ Reduce how much meat and poultry we eat
- ◯ Stick with wild, nontoxic fish

○ Experiment with local food recipes

○ Stash and bring my own bags

○ Install water filter and use reusable bottles—no more bottled water

○ Choose items with less packaging

○ Skip the drive-through and go inside

○ Cut power use in cooking

○ Try canning and freezing surplus local, organic food

○ Cut water use when cleaning

○ Extra credit: Brave composting!

Chapter 4
Sustaining Your Beauty and Mama Earth, page 61

○ Screen products for the "Ugly Fifteen"—use *www.cosmeticsdatabase.com*

○ Discover and choose local, organic products

○ Consider mixing some of your own glamour potions

○ Choose animal-kind products

Chapter 5
Looking Good While Living Local, page 86

○ Push both reuse and recycling across your closets

○ Set up Mama swaps for your family's duds

○ Cut back new purchases. Look for reused goods or recycled materials for all buys.

○ Screen for local, organic, and fair trade manufacturers

○ Do the wash a little less often

○ Wash in cold water with full loads

○ Line dry or consistently clean the dryer's lint screen and use heat sensors.

○ Find my local clean dry cleaner

○ Donate/recycle nonswapped threads, shoes, and gear

○ Rip throwaway clothing items into cleaning rags

Chapter 6
Your Sustainable Home, page 101

○ Set up a varsity recycling plan

○ Organize the neighborhood rummage sale/swap

Save water:

○ Shower: install low-flow shower heads

○ Sinks: install low-flow faucet filters

○ Toilets: place a gallon jug in each tank

○ Washing machine and dishwasher: shorter wash cycles

○ Sprinklers: set up timers and use water sensor sprinklers

Save energy:

○ Appliances: shift to Energy Star when I need new ones

○ CFL lights: swap out the lights as they burn out with CFLs

○ Trap heating/cooling: seal doors and windows, shut chimney flue when not in use

○ Power strips: install at-source to turn off electronics not in use

○ Heat and AC: set temperature at 68 in winter and 74 in summer

Chapter 7
A Mom Needs to Drive: Your Wheels, page 120

- ○ Tighten your driving radius
- ○ Trade one regular drive in your car for a walk or bike ride
- ○ Shift one daily commute to carpool or public transportation
- ○ Drive well: slowly (at the speed limit), smoothly (infrequent stop and starts)
- ○ Maintain your car for better fuel efficiency
- ○ Skip high-grade gasoline unless your car specifically calls for it
- ○ Reduce air travel by two flights per year

Chapter 8
Sustainability at Work, page 135

- ○ Stay local! Find local, sustainable work; telecommute
- ○ Consider shared working environments
- ○ Power strips—install at-the-source power strips to turn off electronics not in use
- ○ Go paperless: don't print; recycle; skip the fax
- ○ Consider Energy Star electronics
- ○ Set up regular electronics recycling

Chapter 9
Staying Lean: Good for You and Your Community, page 148

- ○ Workouts: stay in shape to stay green
- ○ Replace half of your indoor workouts with local, outdoor, or "no earth energy" options (nonelectronic)

○ Shift half of the remaining indoor workouts to elliptical versus treadmill

○ Replace ready-to-retire apparel and gear with recycled items or products made from organic and/or recycled materials

Chapter 10
Family Play Time: Local Leisure, page 157

○ Get smart about local play to-do's

○ Prep with staycation ground-rule planning session

○ Set up home help to minimize chores

○ When you travel, choose sustainable locales and lodging

○ Book sustainable transportation and factor in carbon offsets

Chapter 11
Saving Money and the Earth at the Same Time, page 172

○ Build a family resource allocation plan mapped to your local life priorities: daily expenses, investments, charitable giving, and savings

○ Structure kids' allowance to reflect family priorities

○ Consider investing in small, local business via microfinance

○ Go paperless on banking and bill paying

○ Switch to sustainability-oriented banks and credit cards

Chapter 12
Gift Giving and Holidays: The Ultimate Sustainability Challenge, page 181

○ Recalibrate family holiday traditions and expectations more to "experiences" and less to "things"

○ Organize décor, gift, and clothing swaps

○ Plan menus with an eye to seasonality and locally grown produce

○ Recycle décor and gifts no longer in use

○ Digitize greetings

○ Shift wrapping to reused wrappings, recycled materials, or none at all

Chapter 13
Your Best Friend: Backyard, Sustainable Pet Care, page 201

○ Consider a local shelter to find pets, or support the shelter with donations

○ Revamp pet food, toys, and grooming to meet local and sustainable screens

○ Ensure that pet waste pickup hits sustainability needs

○ If you have an outdoor cat, consider bringing it indoors

Chapter 14
Sustaining the Fun: Media and Entertainment, page 211

○ Replace some screen time with outdoor time

○ Reuse (maintain well) and recycle as much physical media as you can

○ Set up media swaps via your local school and church

○ Mix in more "local life" content

○ Set all media players to power-save mode with at-the-source switches

2

A CRASH COURSE IN LIVING LOCALLY

"True, a little learning is a dangerous thing,
but it still beats total ignorance."

—Abigail Van Buren

Trying to make sense of local options and sustainability guidelines can leave even the most well-informed Mom wondering what to do, how to do it, and what can make the greatest impact in the least amount of time.

Before you begin to examine areas of your life to determine what steps you can take in order to live a more locally focused lifestyle, you need a crash course in what it means to "think sustainability." Throughout the course of this chapter, you'll learn the basics of recycling, the major plastics to avoid, what your carbon footprint is, and how to reduce it.

Easy Recycling in Your Home

Before we dive into the details of how to maximize recycling in your home, please keep top of mind that reducing and reusing both stop purchases before they can happen. Reuse does more for your local community than recycling can. Correctly sorting throwaways is critical, but eliminating the materials and energy used to create a product in the first place trumps recycling the goods every time.

Before I did recycling research, our family recycling endeavors rated as "beginner." We tossed everything deemed "recyclable" into one trash can and threw the bag into the curbside recycling bin. However, because our recycling system lives downstairs in our kitchen and much of what could be recycled was opened upstairs (such as personal care products, toys, and home office items), we missed a lot of things. Not a bad effort, but it turned out to be rather junior varsity.

Luckily, it doesn't take too much work to ramp up recycling. It does take a little advance planning, a trip your local container store, and a review with your household to get everyone on board. With the tips and sources that follow, you can set up your home or office like recycling pros within a day.

RECYCLING PAYS . . . YOU!

Need another reason to recycle? How about discounts good at hundreds of stores like your local Home Depot and CVS? The Recycle Bank has teamed up with retailers to provide discounts based on a recycling load's weight. You can earn more than $500 each year if your local site participates. Find more on *www.recyclebank.com*.

Before getting started, check with your local recycling agency to confirm what can be recycled. Find your community's information via *http://earth911.com*. Sometimes tossing nonrecyclable items into your bin contaminates a whole batch. And, using a black trash bag can get items pulled from the process, since many centers treat all black bags as hazardous waste. Still, if you're unsure, err on the side of recycling. Most services can and will sort out the trash.

Think through your home layout. Set up a designated area to collect common recyclables (cans, paper, plastic) and trash throughout the home. Then set up a specific area for electronics, clothes, and hazardous waste. Hazardous waste includes things like batteries, some hard-core cleaning products, paints, and nail polish remover. I found setting up a dual-bin system (a recycling container and a trash can) in our kitchen, office, bedrooms, and bathrooms made collection convenient. Bed, Bath and Beyond, The Home Depot, The Container Store, and Target all have good, affordable options.

→ Mom to Mom: ←
How to get rid of all that poop?

Did you know most things in landfills never decompose? One of the worst offenders: disposable diapers. They can stick around for more than five hundred years. As my friend Anna, mother of two, put it: "So, if the kids who came over with Christopher Columbus wore diapers, the diapers would still be around today." Check out Chapter 4 for a comparison of recyclable and eco-friendly diapers. No matter your selection, it all just makes a compelling argument to start potty training earlier.

No Recycling Bins?

If your curbside trash pickup does not yet collect recyclables, you can find a center near you at *www.therecyclingcenter.info*, *www.recyclingcenters.org*, or *www.recyclezip.com*. Once you've found a neighboring center, partner with your Mom brigade to start a group recycling program, or take it one step further and get your municipality to bring one on board.

Visit *http://earth911.com* for details on how to start a private program with your Mom's Group, school or neighborhood. Amplify your local initiatives with Mom networks via petitions and letter writing campaigns. By encouraging other moms to get involved, the city is more likely to respond. Work with city council and citizen action groups (search by your state and "citizen action groups" to find organizations near you) to broaden your recycling reach city-wide.

The Nitty Gritty: Recycling 101

So you're ready to upgrade your recycling, but once you dig into the details it seems rather overwhelming. You've heard you can recycle milk cartons, but not all of them; you should recycle paper, but not pizza boxes; or you must recycle glass, but only if it's squeaky clean. Use the cheat sheet below to help you sort out fact from fiction.

General Home

In your home, your recyclables can be broken down into the general categories of aluminum, glass, paper, plastic, and food.

Aluminum is one of the biggest bangs for your recycling buck. Using recycled aluminum saves 95 percent of the energy to make a product versus using new aluminum. To recycle aluminum, simply empty the container and toss in your recycling bin. You earn extra credit for separating aluminum from other materials to ease recyclers' efforts and increase recycling efficiency. You can recycle aerosol cans too. Just pull off the plastic top and make sure to empty the can.

Another recyclable in your home is glass. Virtually immortal, glass can be reused indefinitely. Each reuse saves 20 percent of the greenhouse gases and 50 percent of the water versus producing virgin glass. To recycle glass, lightly clean the container and send to your recycling bin. Don't worry if you don't get every bit of salsa out; most recycling facilities can power-clean your glass. Just like aluminum, you earn extra credit for collecting glass separately, as this saves the recycling facility time and energy.

Between newspapers, direct mail, and product packaging, paper offers a huge recycling opportunity. More than 40 percent of landfill garbage is paper. Using recycled goods saves 95 percent of greenhouse gases, 80 percent of water, and 60 percent of the energy versus using virgin paper. Recycling our Sunday papers alone would save 500,000 trees each week.

The first step in preparing paper and cardboard for recycling is to dry them out, since wet stuff can clog the machines. Then bundle papers and paper products together for recycling.

Did you know you can also recycle books? Pull the hardcovers off of books and recycle the interior pages. Paperbacks can be tossed right into the recycle pile.

Also consider repurposing your favorite magazines and newspapers. When you're finished with your reading, don't use magazines as fire starters—they release toxins as they burn. Recycle them or donate them to a doctor's office (just remember to tear off your subscription information). Or, do as my friend Liz does, and get creative by wrapping presents with your magazines (see page 103 for more eco-gift ideas).

> → **Mom to Mom:** ←
> ## Sustainable Fundraisers
>
> Is your school fundraiser a magazine sales campaign? If you can't swap it for something more eco-friendly like collecting plastic bottles for recycling or selling carbon credits (see page 30 for details), try to add an eco-friendly element. Screen the magazines for those printed on recycled paper. Sell an add-on monthly "recycle" pick up service where kids collect old magazines throughout the neighborhood and donate them to senior centers or hospitals. Or offer subscription sponsorships donating magazines directly to community service centers instead of adding to the home trash bins.

If you look around your home, you'll likely see a lot of plastic. Plastic is the black sheep of materials, and recycling it is paramount. If we recycled just the bottles we use, we'd keep 2 billion tons of toxin-leaching plastic out of landfills. Simply empty and recycle.

Last, while you may not think of food as recyclable, I have one word for you: Compost! Bypass the trash by collecting food scraps and cardboard to help your soil.

Although easy once started, composting can be one of the tougher sustainability initiatives to get going. However, it's such a valuable one on the "reuse" scale, it's worth finding a way to convert. When we first embarked into the land of—well, food decomposition—three other moms and I put a "compost support group" in place to ensure that our sustainability intentions became topsoil realities. Aileen, Danielle, Emily, and I bought composters and e-mailed challenges, solutions, and "output" progress. When Danielle's "compost tea" leaked (ugh), Aileen was quick with a better seal solution. With puffed-out chests, we tout a year of composting under our belts—and can swap the fresh, homegrown veggies to prove it. See the following for tips to increase the ease and decrease the "yuck" factor of home composting.

How to Compost

Composting can be a fascinating home science project or a disgusting stink bomb left out for Mom. My friend Danielle battled bugs, curious dogs, and messy toddlers to get composting in place. She stuck to it and took our friend's Aileen's advice to create a nightly compost competition amongst family members. She now has both a rich herb collection and a clean, green conscience.

Keep composting in the fun zone by investing in easy-to-seal, indoor containers. If you are going to purchase a composter, check out emagineGreen's indoor composter (*www.emagineGreen.com*). It seals tightly so no odors seep out and no critters sneak in. You also can check into the NatureMill Pro Automated Composter (*www.naturemill.com*). You can put dairy and meat products in as well. We use one and find composting as easy as tossing food in the trash can. Or, create your own outdoor compost bin—a box, barrel, or a 2' × 2' backyard area will do it.

Once the compost is ready, you can extend the science project by unloading the "black gold" into a family garden (if you've never gardened, start with herbs and tomatoes—they can be the easiest).

Follow these basic steps to compost:

- Collect food scraps, with the exception of dairy and meat products. Though some composters can handle both dairy and meat, these food scraps can attract animals and other pests.
- Collect nonfood compostables—grass clippings, paper, and cardboard. Exceptions include eucalyptus leaves, poison oak/ivy, and walnuts.
- Add your scraps to the bin, and churn according to the manufacturer's instructions. When the compost is dark and crumbly, add it to the soil.

For more information, see *www.howtocompost.org* and *www.compostguide.com.* Looking to save money while composting? Many counties offer discounts on home kits, and also take grass-clipping donations.

Special Handling

Of course, there are some items around your house that you'll want to rid yourself of without putting the burden on your local landfill. So what to do with those lingering things? Read on.

Appliances are big and bulky, but they have a lot to offer in second lives. Rule of thumb: You can recycle your appliance if it's more than

50 percent metal. Send your appliances on to a better place via local shelter donations or bulk recycling. Try *www.recycle-steel.org*.

Ripping up your carpeting? Don't toss it in the dumpster. First try to repurpose it. Does the kids' tree fort or garage workshop need a new floor covering? How about a better kennel for your furry friends? If you still have carpet remaining, it can be easy to donate or send on as long as it's dry. There are many places that will whisk your carpets away; see *www.carpetrecovery.org*. You also can check with the manufacturer to see if they will accept it. Companies including Flor, Milliken, and Shaw do.

If you're like many moms, you have drawers and closets full of clothes and shoes, only half of which you wear. Set aside the grin-inducing items for children's dress-up and Halloween costumes. Then purge the closets and bag up the rest for local shelter donations. Most folks appreciate a clean garment, but extending a garment's longevity via dirty donations still beats trashed threads. Check out Goodwill, the Salvation Army, or local charities to find out where your used duds will be best put to use.

We tread within a plugged-in, battery-operated world. Ease your device impact on the earth by recycling your electronics when you move on to the next hot gadget. Many manufacturers are making it easier for us to do the right thing. If the manufacturer doesn't have an option, you can try several websites for easy electronics eco-paths. For a national list of electronics' second (or third) homes, see *www.recycles.org*. Check with *www.recycleforbreastcancer.com* to donate your items to help raise money for a good cause. If you have DVDs and video games you've watched or played enough, try *www .greendisk.com*. See Chapter 14 for more media ideas.

With all your gadgets coming and going, you likely have quite the stash of chargers and batteries at any given time. Because these batteries have toxins such as mercury, they're hazardous waste. Put them in a biodegradable bag or even an old plastic bag and take them to Radio Shack, Office Depot, or your hazardous waste facility. You can also try recycling rechargeable batteries by signing up at *www .call2recycle.org*. Ship batteries to them and they do the work. Or, if you're lucky enough to live near a Whole Foods grocery store, most will take both alkaline and rechargeable batteries and recycle them for you. Then, shift to rechargeable batteries. *Note: Recycle car batteries by returning them to a retailer who sells them. Most contain lead and should not hit landfills lest they leach the toxin.*

If you're upgrading your cell phone and need to get rid of your older model, you can find manufacturing programs in place through various cell phone stores such as AT&T and Nokia. Or, you can donate or recycle your phone. Visit Greenphone.com or Recyclewireless phones.com for more information. Also remember Cellphonesfor soldiers.org for a good cause.

Many computer and printer manufacturers now have recycling programs. Contact them directly to find out how to recycle your system. Also look into recycling programs through electronics retailers, or consider donating the equipment. Visit *www.nextsteprecycling .org* for details. Or, try MyGreenElectronics.org for more options. To convert electronics to a good cause, visit *www.cristina.org* or *www .sharetechnology.org*. They refurbish your gadgets and donate them to organizations in need.

If you wear eyeglasses and your prescription has changed or you're simply updating your look, don't just toss those old ones in a drawer. For your own version of second sight, share your global view by recycling your lens. See *www.neweyesfortheneedy.org*. Or check with *www.onesight.org* for participating doctors and stores such as Target who'll recycle your shades.

If you have medications (prescription or over the counter) that you no longer need, many pharmacies and doctor's offices will dispose of your leftovers. If yours won't, take old medications to the hazardous waste facility. When you don't, they end up leaching into the earth through landfills or spiking our drinking water as you flush those cares away.

Are your kids constantly tossing out almost-empty glue containers and asking for new crayons because theirs are broken? No problem. Clean out glue containers and send them to a second life via *www .elmersgluecrew.com*. Send crayons on to *www.crazycrayons.com*. You can leave the wrapper on, and you don't have to worry about broken little crayon nubs—they melt the crayons and make new ones.

Apparently many major retailers haven't gotten the sustainability message—if you order something through the mail, even today, you're likely to get an added "bonus" with your item: packing peanuts. Once you've peeled their little static-clingy selves off your hands, clothes, and everything else within a one-foot radius of your package, collect and box 'em up and out. You can recycle them at *www.loosefillpackaging.com*.

Anyone who has done any painting around the house most likely has half-empty paint cans cluttering the garage and releasing volatile organic compounds (VOCs). If you're itching to get the cans out of your garage, seal them shut and take them to your local hazardous waste dump. Find the closest one at *http://earth911.com*. For latex paint, let it dry out, seal the container, and put it in your regular trash collection. Then see Chapter 6 for eco-friendly paint recommendations.

Something that certainly can't be tossed into your recycle bin is your car. If you're looking to donate a vehicle, keep in mind that most Goodwill and Salvation Army locations will take the car while you get a tax deduction. Tax laws on the deduction value are ever-changing and vary state by state. When estimating what a vehicle write-off would be worth, keep in mind that the IRS no longer allows you take the "Blue Book" (Kelley Blue Book) value of your vehicle as your deduction. Instead, you take the actual sales value or auction price of your vehicle as your deduction. Visit VehiclesforCharity.org for more details, and be sure to follow the IRS guidelines surrounding car donation. You can find the latest IRS guidelines on *www.irs.gov*.

Getting rid of your tires? Though it may cost you $1–$5 per tire, it's worth the time and money to recycle your treads. Check out *www.epa.gov* for locations.

Do you change your own oil? Good for you. But what do you do with the mucky brown used oil? I hope you don't dump it down the drain. Since motor oil contains heavy metals and toxins, it's hazardous waste. Do not dump it. Recycle instead. Put used oil in a plastic or glass container (like a milk jug). Mark it as "used motor oil" and take it to your local recycling or hazardous waste location or your local service station. Most chains like Grand Auto, Jiffy Lube, Pep Boys, Valvoline, or Walmart will also take your oil.

Come across mysterious items when cleaning out the garage for the block party rummage sale? If you don't know what something is or where to send it, pack it up for hazardous waste. Find your local center at *www.epa.gov*.

Packing up small, everyday items such as batteries or CFL light bulbs can be a nuisance. Set up a biodegradable trash bag (available in most grocery stores) on the back of a hall closet door on each floor in your house. It's easier to remember to toss the small items there and pick up the bag as part of your weekly trash takeout chore. Add weekly bags to a cardboard box to keep collecting hazardous waste until you're ready to visit the local facility. Otherwise, kids (and grownups) may give in to the temptation to toss a battery in the trash "just this one time." For the big items, do a quarterly home "purge"

including hazardous waste, large items to recycle, and clothes/gear/
toy clean-outs. A reminder: please treat CFLs bulbs as hazardous
waste since they contain trace amounts of mercury.

When recycling, there are a few don'ts to remember:

- Try not to put any food or overly soiled containers (like pizza
  boxes) with other items to be recycled.
- Do not include dirty diapers or anything with human or pet
  waste.
- Separate hazardous items such as paints, many carpets, foam
  padding, and oilcans.
- Most centers do not accept mirrors, latex, rubber, or steel items.

UpCycling: Moms Turn to Fundraising

Want a new way to raise money for your child's school or Brownie
troop? Try an amped-up version of recycling: upcycling. The new,
new way to recycle, upcycling (the word was coined by *Cradle to
Cradle* authors William McDonough and Michael Braungart) creates
new products from waste. Companies such as TerraCycle pay a
bounty (about two cents per piece) for specific items, which they
in turn convert from trash to treasure. Take the lead to sign up your
organization and collect everything from Oreo cookie wrappers (of
course they're someone else's) to Capri Sun juice bags. TerraCycle
runs a myriad of different collection "brigades": bags, plastic bottles,
yogurt containers, packaging from cookies, chips, and energy bars,
and—here's a way to put girls' night out to a good cause—wine
corks!

TerraCycle reincarnates your trash into school supplies, hip bags,
fire logs, garden supplies, and cleaning products. All you have to
do is mail in the goods via a prepaid shipping label the company
provides.

Extend the upcycling trend by creating your own treasures from trash and selling them as a fundraiser. Sites like CraftStylish.com, CraftingaGreenworld.com, and Ehow.com offer relatively easy-to-do and marketable project ideas.

Purging Plastics Without Sacrifice

We make almost five times more plastic than we did ten years ago—70 billion pounds versus 15 billion pounds. The bottled water industry alone drove half of plastic production's increase. Since plastic recycling rates have stayed relatively constant during this same time period, we're tossing five times as much plastic into our landfills, waterways, and ecosystems. Because we recycle less than 20 percent of it, plastic makes up 80 percent of our ocean trash and 35 percent of our landfill trash. Many plastics are just poisons in disguise (see page 23). A shift away from plastics puts your sustainability journey on the fast track.

Avoiding plastics often surfaces as a sustainability theme. Why? Because the ingredients in most plastics make them tough on the world when they're made, tough on you as you use them, and tough on the earth's disposal system.

Plastics come mostly from fossil fuels and synthetic chemicals. Many raw ingredients used to make plastics are scarce. Also, the manufacturing process burns a disproportionate share of energy and water while leaving behind a bundle of toxic waste.

Much of what makes up fossil fuels and synthetic chemicals has been linked to cancer, nerve damage, and organ failure. Though we don't directly eat plastic, its materials enter our bodies through our mouth and skin via food, water, and gear. Avoiding plastics may prove impossible, but reducing exposure by choosing glass or organic fibers helps. And remember: never heat food or beverages in plastic. Heat facilitates the bad stuff getting into your good stuff.

Eighty percent of plastics head to landfills instead of recycling bins. Adding to landfill mass is one downside. Even worse, plastics don't biodegrade efficiently, so the toxins travel back into our ecosystem.

Plastic products carry recycling ratings #1–#7. A summary of these ratings, their definitions, and a description of the products follow. Your biggest health and environment watch-outs are coded for recycling as #3, #6, and #7.

THE SEVEN TYPES OF PLASTIC

1. *PET (polyethylene terephthalate).* Less damaging, you'll find this plastic mostly in drink containers, fast-food containers, and microwave or oven-prepared frozen dinners. It's also commonly found in peanut butter and jelly containers.

2. *HDPE (high-density polyethylene).* As you pick up these containers, you'll note a heavier feel. You'll find # 2 plastic mostly used for household cleaners; laundry detergent bottles; milk containers; juice bottles; cracker, cereal, and cookie liners; and many grocery, retailer, or trash bags. It also is found in personal care packaging for products like shampoo and makeup.

3. *PVC (polyvinyl chloride, or vinyl).* Yikes! PVC, The most poisonous of the plastic poisons, shows up everywhere. You're carrying PVC around in backpacks, food storage containers, and notebook binders. It's common in shower curtains, clingy plastic wraps, and in the tops of some glass bottles (like olive oil and salad dressing bottles). PVC has received a lot of press for its use in toys and electronic packaging—think of those impossible-to-open "blister packs" and "clam shells." "Big box" retailers such as Walmart and Costco have been working with suppliers to reduce the number of products that use PVC in their packaging.

4. *LDPE (low-density polyethylene).* This plastic is found in thin bags such as those used for veggies, sliced bread, frozen fruit and veggies, and dry cleaning, as well as on paper milk carton coatings or in squeezable mayo, honey, and mustard bottles.

5. *PP (polypropylene).* This is a common grocery product plastic used in things such as ketchup bottles, horseradish containers, and sour cream and butter containers, as well as medicine bottles and drinking straws.

6. *PS (polystyrene).* Another "yikes." Styrene is a no-no. Styrene leaches into the food and beverages you consume. According to the EPA, "short-term styrene exposure at levels above the Maximum Contaminant Level (used to set drinking water standards) can cause nervous system effects such as a loss of concentration, weakness, and nausea. Long-term exposure can cause liver and nerve damage and cancer." You'll find # 6 PS in CD jackets, food-service items, meat and poultry trays, egg cartons, aspirin bottles, packing peanuts, plastic tableware, coat hangers, videocassettes, and some toys.

7. *"Other."* Although this is a bit of a catchall classification number, the "all other" category marking often identifies products made with polycarbonates such as Bisphenol-A (BPA), which is an endocrine impactor. BPA received a lot of press and was recently scrutinized for removal from baby bottles and drinking bottles. More than 80 percent of published studies regarding low-dose BPA exposure on lab animals found scary effects. Male and female infertility, changes to brain chemistry, and degradation to the immune system all turned up across the studies. The #7 plastic is used in metal food can liners, sport water bottles, and many baby bottles, as well as a myriad of other items. Opt for glass baby bottles or BPA-free bottles. Try Born Free or Green to Grow for bottles and sip cups. For sport bottles,

choose from an ever-increasing set of Nalgene bottles designs. And, if you must buy bottled water, recycle your bottle and look for new-looking bottles, rather than scratched or scuffed bottles.

Purge the PVC

Look for the #3 or a "V" for products to avoid. PVC is especially rough since its production spews dioxins and other carcinogens. Manufacturers soften PVC via chemicals (phthalates, adipates) known as plasticizers. Studies link PVC to neural, developmental, and reproductive defects as well as kidney and liver damage. Plasticizers leach into products during use and—since PVC doesn't recycle easily—it sits in landfills leaking plasticizer toxins into soil and waterways postconsumption.

If you're using PVC products, avoid chemical leaching: keep products out of the heat, since heat breaks down ingredients and accelerates transferring PVCs. Always keep PVC items away from food and drink. Ready to go on a PVC hunt? It's scary how pervasive the plastic is, but you can sniff it out (often literally) and move it out of your home:

- In your closets: Pull out backpacks, handbags, boots, luggage, raincoats, shoes, and watchbands and check for the PVC symbols, or take a deep breath for that signature plastic-y smell.
- In your furnishings and décor: Check mattress pads, imitation leather furniture, plastic Christmas trees, photo albums, strollers, shower curtains, and toys—especially when children are still young enough to put toys in their mouths.
- In your kitchen: Try to replace food storage containers, baby bottles, drinking cups and straws, dish drying racks, plastic food wrap, plastic utensils, and tablecloths. Alternate materials are glass, fabric, and bamboo for these items.

- In your office: Check clipboards, notebooks, plastic paper clips, plastic folders, some staple containers, and some types of tape.
- In the great outdoors: PVC sneaks into balls, garden hoses, inflatable swimming pools, inflatable furniture, riding toys, and tarps.

Although it seems PVC is everywhere, you can dial back your family's exposure if not completely eliminate it. Many manufacturers are working to make non-PVC versions of common products, or at a minimum are pulling out phthalates. Need more options? The Center for Health, Environment and Justice has a list of safe, PVC-free alternative products. Visit its website at *www.chej.org.*

Now that you've got the basics down, you're ready to craft your personal "Busy Mom's Family Go-Green Plan."

Building Your Family Happy-Go-Local Action Plan

To translate local living ideas into everyday life, review chapter tips and recommendations and note suggestions that best match your family's needs and your eco-goals. Start with the action item summary that follows. Check off tips you're interested in trying and then check them off as complete in the months ahead. As you read chapter details, add notes on favorite product and resource ideas alongside the tips.

Chore List

Older kids can help with recycling, composting, organizing monthly home "clean sweeps," and researching and choosing local versions of supplies or gear for their activities, as well as getting involved in local environmental nonprofits. Even younger kids can learn to do things like throwing certain items in the recycling versus the trash can, selecting toys for donations, or helping to choose and cook organic foods.

Set up and post Family Sustainability Targets for saving water and energy and adding eco-products into your day-to-day routine. Have some fun with a weekly family review to check in on all initiatives. Put rewards in place for milestones you hit and measurable energy and dollar savings goals.

→ Mom to Mom: ←
Make It a Family Plan

Avoid adding another category of to-do's to your already too-long list by building a "Family Sustainability Plan" instead of "Mom's Plan." Spend family time sorting through possible changes and committing to try a few each month. Once you have determined your family's top actions, integrate them into your day-to-day life through kid's chore lists, allowances, and your home savings plan. For examples of chore lists, allowance guidelines, and savings plans, flip to page 27.

Allowances

Rewire your kids' allowances to incorporate long-term-thinking ideas like giving back to the local community, building a savings account, and supporting earth-friendly goals. If you tie allowances to a chore list, make sure you add the family local life to-do's to the list. You can also motivate more sustainable behavior via "allowance bonuses" or "refunds" for a percentage of avoided purchases, or reuse and recycling options.

Savings Plan

Convincing everyone in the house to embrace a locally focused plan may be tough. Some just don't buy in (yet) to the idea that the state of our world right now really does threaten the future of the lifestyle we know and enjoy. For those folks, try the savings plan angle. Look for the price tag (🏷️) alongside money-saving tips and product recommendations in this book. Add those into your family plan, set a savings target, and start measuring money banked due to your green living.

What's My Carbon Footprint? And Why Should I Care?

Your carbon footprint equals how many tons of greenhouse gases (GHGs) you emit into the atmosphere via day-to-day activities. This metric matters, since an increase in GHG emissions results in a decrease in the earth's sustainability. Greenhouse gases trap energy in the earth's atmosphere, thus heating us up. GHGs include carbon dioxide, hydrofluorocarbons, methane, nitrous oxide, perfluorocarbons, and sulfur hexafluoride. As you shift to more local consumption, you help reduce GHG emissions by reducing things such as transportation emissions.

The term "carbon footprint" refers to the fact that carbon dioxide makes up more than 80 percent of human-made GHG emissions. However, the calculation of your carbon footprint reflects all greenhouse gases associated with your lifestyle and may be communicated as CO_2e, or carbon dioxide equivalent units. Although other metrics exist, your carbon footprint has become the most common way to quantify your impact on your environment.

To be precise, a carbon footprint would include an allocated cost of all the things you do. For example, your morning java carbon charge would include the cost of making your coffee, transporting it to your grocery store, and supplying the energy to power the store *plus* your direct costs of bringing the coffee home, storing it, and then brewing your cup.

In more practical terms, your footprint is usually calculated based on your home (its size and location) and your transportation habits

(what type of car you drive, how much mileage you average per year, and how often you travel via airplane).

The United States per-person greenhouse gas emission level is about twenty tons per year. On average, the activities we choose to do make up about half of that, so the average American's "controllable" carbon footprint would be ten tons per year. In the United States, transportation, specifically cars, makes up 30 percent of all CO_2 emissions.

So, why should you care what your carbon footprint is? By knowing your carbon footprint and working to reduce it, you have a quantifiable tool to measure the impact of your family's local and sustainable efforts. With most studies ranking America as number one or two in terms of per-person greenhouse gas emissions worldwide, we have room to improve.

The concept of being "carbon neutral" or offsetting your emissions comes from a relatively recent market phenomenon wherein companies or large-scale projects receive incentives to reduce their direct GHG emissions.

→ Mom to Mom: ←
Find Your Family Footprint

For a compelling, kid-friendly picture, calculate your family's "ecological footprint." This shows how many earths we'd need if everyone on the planet lived your family's lifestyle. After calculating ours (more than one world and less than five—yikes!), I went straight to Climate Trust and did not pass go. Visit *www.ecofoot.org*.

When an organization works to make fewer GHGs, the difference between its emission counts before and after any materials or process changes creates carbon credits, called Certified Emissions Reductions

(CERs). The organization or an aggregator can then "resell" those CERs to people wanting to counter their carbon footprint impact.

Buying CERs or "ozone credits" equal to your carbon footprint can neutralize eco-sins. You can also skip the CER market and donate directly to an organization working to build renewable energy sources or clean up our planet (see page 176 for options).

How Do I Find Out My Carbon Footprint?

Many websites can calculate your footprint based the broad input mentioned in the previous section (your home, your car, and your travel habits). A general number may be enough to shoot for as you try to neutralize your impact.

But, if you'd like a deeper level of detail, try *www.carboncount.org*, *www.nature.org*, and *www.climatecrisis.net* (site home for the film *An Inconvenient Truth*).

Once you know your footprint, you can help offset it through a number of companies that sell CERs. The Clean Air Planet Group reviewed thirty resellers and highlighted eight as top-tier. Three U.S.-based companies—*www.tufts.edu/tie/tci/carbononoffsets/index.htm*, *www.climatetrust.org*, *and www.nativenergy.com*—cleared the group's screen.

Visit *www.climatecounts.org* for a comparison of how companies stack up on the carbon counts. There are also a number of sites that allow you to address specific elements of your carbon impact, such as a vacation or transportation. Try *www.TerraPass.com*, *www.SustainableTravelInternational.org*, and *www.BetterWorldClub.com.* Find a more comprehensive list at *www.treehugger.com*.

"We must be the change we wish to see in the world."
—Mahatma Gandhi

KEEPING YOUR FAMILY'S FOOD AND DRINK LOCAL, SUSTAINABLE, AND HEALTHY

> "Nothing would be more tiresome than eating and drinking if God had not made them a pleasure as well as a necessity."
>
> —Voltaire

Our kitchens are often the center of our home life. Tackle one of the most far-reaching areas of your family's local life plan by restocking shelves, simplifying cleaning routines, and cleaning up food storage. If you're overwhelmed by the price of local or organic products, remember that farmers' markets, CSAs, and co-ops offer a vast selection of locally grown goods without mass-market overhead baked into the prices. Independent markets and corner stores are often stocked with local goods. Ask the grocer about them, or search for local labels on their shelves.

EYE OPENERS
- The average meal travels between 1,500 and 2,500 miles before it gets to your plate.
- Farmers' markets help farmers keep eighty to ninety cents of each dollar that you spend versus the six cents of every dollar that conventional farmers earn.

The Sustainability Screen: Food and Drink

Change the World

1. Start Here!

Eat and drink less

Shop your local farmers' markets and join a CSA

Skip bottled water—install filters and stock up on reusable bottles

Always bring your own bags

Choose fewer packaged and disposable items

Cook in the microwave

Cook with pot covers

Use parchment paper or aluminum foil instead of plastic wrap

3. Reach For It!

"Adopt" a farmer

Grow key produce and herbs

Eat less meat (and chicken)

Compost

Buy what's fresh and freeze it for later

Use glass for storage instead of plastic

Swap out appliances for Energy Star versions

Buy cheese in blocks and slice/grate

IMPACT

2. Why Not?

Buy fresh fish instead of farmed

Buy fresh foods, then frozen, then canned

Request no napkins or cutlery when taking out food

Reuse water—boil it or water plants

Load the dishwasher completely

Wash in cold water with short cycles

Skip the drive-through

Use recycled paper products

4. Save for Last!

Grow all your own food

Add in a chicken coop

Recycle rainwater for home use

Use a rain barrel to store water for longer-term use

Shift to a vegetarian diet

Baby Steps Count

Simple   **EASE TO DO**   Disruptive

- Despite a national obesity rate of 60 percent in America, we throw away 30 percent of the food we buy, which adds up to 163 pounds per person per year, or $600 per home. That's enough to feed 49 million hungry people.
- Our children average 50 to 90 pounds of lunch-box waste per year.
- Our schools throw out more than 12 percent of the food they make, at a cost of $300 million.

THE LOCAL-LIFE GUIDELINES FOR HEALTHY FOOD AND DRINK

1. *Shopping mantra:* Buy none, buy less, buy used, buy local.
2. *Buy local, organic, and fair trade:* You are what you eat.
3. *Eat less meat:* A few more vegetables are good for you and your wide open spaces.
4. *Eat the right fish:* Get straight on screening for toxicity impacting you as well as the earth.
5. *Give up bottled water:* Save the planet and your money.
6. *Bring your own bags:* Plastic or paper? Neither. Bring a reusable bag instead.
7. *Choose less packaging:* Skip veggie bags, buy in bulk, and reuse what you've got.
8. *Sustainable food prep:* The proper cooking and storage techniques can save energy, water, and time.
9. *Sustainable cleanup:* Use less water and more eco-friendly dishwashing soaps.
10. *Takeout:* Get your to-go order without napkins, Styrofoam, and disposable cutlery.
11. *Eat out:* Pick nearby places that prepare local food and serve smaller portions.

Best Bets For Food and Drink

As you tighten your screen on what to feed your family, labels can be a valuable shortcut or a misleading marketing claim. Look for third-party verification of any label. Review by an outside organization keeps claim definitions consistent, and claims a wee bit more honest. Some of the most common third-party verified claims include:

USDA Organic: no hormones, antibiotics, pesticides, genetic engineering; certified sustainable farming practices
Food Alliance: low or no pesticides, fair work conditions, habitat protection, and well-managed production processes
Healthy Grown: low pesticide
Fair Trade Certified: fair working conditions, eco-farming, and community support
100% Natural: products do not contain synthetic ingredients or artificial flavors, colors, or preservatives.

Less common third-party-verified labels that may hit your grocery shopping screen address meat, fish, and poultry. Such labels include:

Grass-Fed or Pastured: diet of natural forage outdoors
rBGH Free: cows had no growth hormones
Certified Humane Raised and Handled: pastured and humane care of livestock
Demeter Biodynamic: no synthetic pesticides; pastured livestock and well-managed agricultural practices
Wild Caught: caught during the legal fishing season in the wild
Marine Stewardship Council: certifies "well-managed" fisheries
Salmon Safe: products (which could interestingly include beer, cheese, and produce) that were produced while protecting watersheds and salmon habitats

> ## Mom to Mom:
> ## Caffeine Fix
>
> Want to caffeine-up guilt free? Even if you don't live where the java bean grows, you can find local roasters. In a pinch, look for USDA Organic, Fair Trade Certified, and Bird Friendly (coffee grown under shade trees to preserve birds' habitat) on your bag of beans.
>
> As a final sustainable seal of approval, the bag may also carry the logo of The Rainforest Alliance (which means the product was sourced in a way that keeps rainforests sustainable) and the Green Seal, which confirms that the product has a low environmental impact (applies to cleaners, paints, and papers as well).

Labels to double-check or read with care include those that don't require any third-party verification. Many meat and poultry producers make claims such as "Antibiotic or Hormone Free," "Free Range," "Fresh," or "Natural." These claims may indeed be true, but no oversight group has defined consistent guidelines or confirmed that the products met any marketed claim. All of these labels and claims spinning your head? You can sidestep them while going as local as can be by growing your own food.

More details follow, but your Best Bet food and drink resources are these:

www.sustainabletable.org
www.ota.orgwww.organicconsumers.org
www.centerforfoodsafety.org
www.coopamerica.org
www.emagineGreen.com for BPA-free plastic and aluminum bottles
Born Free and Green to Grow for BPA-free baby bottles
www.100milediet.org: find food within 100 miles of where you live

www.ams.usda.gov/FARMERSMARKETS/
www.farmersmarket.com
www.localharvest.org
www.dinegreen.com

The Nitty Gritty: Your Food and Drink

For many of us, eating seems complicated enough without having to factor in local and sustainability issues. Good news: you can easily find food options to keep you and your community lean and green. For your local living, eco-friendly feast plan, follow these Local Life Guidelines:

Buy None, Buy Less, Buy Used, Buy Local

While some of this may be hard to achieve, your food shopping mantra should once again focus on *buy none, buy less, buy used, buy local*. Though it takes some effort, it is not impossible to achieve.

"Buy none" may be tough to do, but it can be doable with the most local of all locations—your very own garden. If growing *everything* you eat feels a bit overwhelming, start small. Growing a tomato plant or a window basket of herbs lies within reach for all of us.

Since we throw away a third of the food we buy, "buy less" is clearly doable. As a society battling high obesity levels, some abstinence could do us—and the world—pounds of good. On the sustainability scale, there's a bit of a tradeoff between buying bulk to save packaging and buying smaller sizes that meet our real needs. In the end, buying less trumps all else. We can all win on a personal and community level by eating and drinking less.

As far as buying used, this one is simple: eat your leftovers. If you find yourself consistently throwing out leftovers, rethink the amount of food you prepare and consider freezing the unused portions. It will save you time, money, and waste.

As for "buy local," this one leads us to the bulk of our Local Life Guidelines.

Buy Local and Buy Sustainable

When I first began learning about "being local," there seemed to be as many definitions for local as there were local municipalities. Local was anything within 1,500 miles of your home. No, 250 miles. No; to be *truly* local things must be within 100 miles of your home. This confused me and seemed a bit unobtainable. I live in the midst of densely populated suburbia. I can find just about anything I need within 10 miles of my home, but things actually *made* within 100 miles of my home? Beyond farmers' markets, chances seemed slim.

However, digesting more locavore lore, I came to understand that buying "local" really just comes down to targeting as many close-to-home products as you can. For some gifted gardeners (which I am not), this means growing most of your produce. For other brave-hearts in appropriately zoned neighborhoods, adding one or two chickens to a coop in the yard becomes an option. But for most of us, increasing our supply of local goods translates into shopping locally managed stores, visiting farmers' markets, signing up for local CSAs (detailed in the following section), exchanging homemade goods, and choosing locally owned restaurants dishing up local produce.

Once you broaden your local scope from "what's grown in my backyard" to "what's made in my town," you'll be surprised at how many local options exist. Look for local canned and baked goods manufacturers, brew pubs, premade gourmet meal suppliers, or confectioners. Sample your local sandwich and coffee shops for eat-there treats as well as items to add to your pantry. Even national grocery chains may stock locally made bakery and deli goods, local canned goods and, of course, nearby farmers' produce. As you increase the share of "local" goods on your shopping lists, expand your buying screen to address "buying sustainable." Buying sustainable boils down to buying things that have been made and delivered in a way that supports our earth's long-term viability. Lessons learned in recent years on how to be "green" make being "sustainable" feel very familiar. Look for items with earth-friendly ingredients and manufacturing processes. Remember to incorporate sustainable processes into your home cooking, cleaning, and storing routines. There are many choices and options; review the following tips to see what fits best into your family lifestyle.

Buy Local and Organic

Before we get into how to find food that meets the local life screen, let's put a little bit of thought into why it's worth buying things that are locally grown and/or organically made in terms of your personal sustainability. When it comes to food, the bottom line is this: when possible, buy local and look for the USDA Organic seal. If you would like to achieve the healthiest lifestyle possible, you absolutely must eat clean, local, and/or organic. It's that simple.

I once sat next to a neurosurgeon at a wedding reception. Initiating the requisite banter, I asked what was the single most important thing I could do to keep my brain healthy. I expected to hear about daily Sudoku puzzles, changing up my routines, and getting regular exercise.

Instead he answered quite simply: Eat, drink, and use organic products. The biggest contributor to brain decay is cell destruction. To reduce cell destruction, reduce your toxin intake. Since you can't immediately change what's in the air, be vigilant about what you ingest and absorb. Only eat, drink, and use products made without pesticides, hormones, and additives.

In your quest to set a local table, keep your focus on buying products from manufacturers near your home. If you can't have both

local and organic, which way to go? Lean toward local. Odds are, the food has been made on a smaller scale, providing 98 percent of the benefits of certified organic foods for only 2 percent of the fuel and transportation costs/energy used to get non-local food to the store.

Whenever you run into roadblocks sourcing local treats, come back to the top five reasons for bothering:

1. Yum! Locally grown food tastes better. Don't believe it? Try those samples at the farmers' market. Delicious!
2. Invest in your economy. Support your local tax base and your neighbors. Buy products made in your town.
3. It's better for you. Because local produce gets to you quickly, it ripens longer and stays fresher, retaining more nutrients than conventionally grown items.
4. Sustain, sustain, sustain. Earth-friendly farming and reduced transportation—long live the earth!
5. Save money. Without the overhead of conventional farm companies, local growers often can offer lower prices despite their smaller scale.

To find local produce, try your local community supported agriculture (CSA) program. CSAs enable you to buy a season's worth of local farmers' produce. The site *www.Localharvest.org* lists local farmers and CSAs by city and state. You may also visit *www.farmfreshtoyou.com* for home deliveries of local farmers' goods.

The National Sustainable Agriculture website (*www.attra.org*) lists local food sources by state. You can also search for local farms as well as co-ops. Want to know what's in season or about to be? To find seasonal produce near you, visit *www.sustainableharvest.org*. The site has a seasonal search engine synced to your Zip Code and the time of year. You can also visit *www.seasonalrecipes.com* for seasonal produce as well as recipes. Of course, iPhone also can come to the rescue. Download locavore 2.0 (paid app) to get real-time data about what's in season in your neck of the woods.

→ **Mom to Mom:** ←
More Veggies than You Can Cook?

Many CSA baskets embody the cornucopia-runneth-over mentality. So many colorful, exotic veggies and fruits, but not enough of a household or days in the week to put them all to use before spoilage sets in . . . mmm, what's a sustainable living, waste-not mom to do? Double (or even triple) up. I split a bi-weekly basket with Marilyn, a neighboring mom. We seem to be well matched; my husband devours the onions that her husband scorns, and hers feasts on the beans mine won't touch. Plenty of healthy eating, creative cooking, and local living going on with zero waste.

While you're getting to know your local CSAs and farmers' markets, consider "adopting" a local farmer and forging a family relationship by frequenting the farmer's stands, aggregating the produce for your neighbors, and touring the farm facilities.

Feeling inspired (or brave) enough to go hard-core local? If you want to try to stay within a 100-mile radius, visit *www.100milediet .org*. The site has a calculator to help you define your shopping options as well as a myriad of restaurant, farmers' markets, and CSA locators.

In addition to sidestepping poisons, choosing local and organic products means supporting sustainable farming and manufacturing processes. In comparison to conventional farming and production, organic farming uses fewer resources, emits less toxic waste, and leaves the land in better shape. This leaves the earth in a better state to continue working with us for what we'll need in generations to come. Go to *www.organicconsumers.org* for more information.

If you'd like to connect with nearby locavores, check out *www.foodroutes.org* and visit the Buy Fresh Buy Local tab for local chapter information. The organization has local chapters in most states, with more opening monthly. For detailed information and some of most committed locavore perspective, visit *www.hyperlocavore.com.*

One additional watch-out: Skip genetically engineered (GE) foods. According to the Center For Food Safety, "70–75 percent of processed foods on supermarket shelves—from soda to soup, crackers to condiments—contain genetically engineered ingredient." In addition to processed foods, GE foods pop up in almost all produce as well as basic-ingredient crops such as wheat. Many experts link the ingredients and processes required to engineer food to long-term health issues. No consistent regulation or labeling for GE foods exists yet, though much is in the works. To be safe, stick with local and organic food and drink to the greatest extent possible. For details, see *www.foodsafetynow.org.* To check your foods by brand for genetically engineered ingredients, visit *www.truefoodnow.org* and search the site for "printable shopper's guide" to download a cheat sheet.

Want to get a local life star plus extra-credit points? Buy Fair Trade Certified products. These goods are made in fair working conditions through community building programs and environmentally sustainable production processes. Currently, certification is available for certain U.S. goods: coffee and tea, herbs, fresh fruit, sugar, and various other staples such as rice and—every busy mom's staple—chocolate.

You can find Fair Trade Certified products at restaurants and retailers including Ben & Jerry's Scoop Shops, Dunkin' Donuts, Seattle's Best Coffee, and Starbucks. If you'd like to read more about why local, organic, and fair trade processes are so important to your health and the earth's longevity, visit the Organic Trade Association's website at *www.ota.com.*

Local and Organic Champagne Feasts on a Beer Budget

Does the idea of buying local and organic *everything* make your wallet shudder? True, historically, many local and organic items tended to cost a bit more. Larger-scale production and distribution methods now are changing that balance, so the most critical items are close to or on par with the price of conventional products. In addition, many grocery stores are sourcing local suppliers across categories as well as investing in their own private-label organic items to shave even more off the price.

Still, if the price of going 100 percent local and/or organic scares you, here are a few tips to bridge the gap:

- For fresh produce, stick to the top twelve on page 47 as your organic must-haves.
- Remember that frozen can be as good as fresh and often costs less.
- Explore freezing and canning fresh fruits and veggies yourself at home (see sources below).

Note: Imported brands do not have to meet USDA standards to be labeled organic in their own countries. Most countries do have solid organic standards, but be aware. Also, water, fish, and salt cannot be labeled organic.

Buy Less Meat

Study after study hammers home the point: the single most local-living, sustainability-oriented, eco-friendly food choice you can make is to eat less meat. That's painful for the cheeseburger-loving Texan

I am, but true all the same. Meat, poultry, and fish all require some mix of land, water, energy, pesticides, antibiotics, and—the worst—massive fecal-waste management. Plus, the conventional ranch and farm conditions are flat-out foul. There is nothing "local" about mass-market livestock management and processing.

In order to understand why it's so important to shift from processed meat and poultry to local produce (best case) or independently managed, antibiotic-free livestock, consider that half of all the water we consume as a nation is used to grow grain for cattle feed.

Since 80 percent of U.S. agricultural land is used for meat production, a drop in meat consumption could free up our collective backyard for better uses. I'm betting your community could think of more than a few ways to repurpose at least one acre of the 260 million acres of U.S. forest that have been cleared to grow crops for livestock.

For an even more compelling way to share the meat story with your family, watch the short animated videos in The Meatrix Series (www.themeatrix.com). I hear you sigh. I understand. I can't completely swear off blue-cheese burgers and chicken salad. But, cut back? Definitely can do. You too?

Cutting back on meat brings up another issue: to fish-feast or not to fish-feast? That is the question, at least for a person striving to be both fit and fish-friendly. You probably know to avoid fish farms (where fish live among a disturbingly high density of their own feces) as well as mercury (see sidebar). Find out which fish are the best for you—and your local waterways—at *www.edf.org.*

For a quick answer, try the Blue Ocean Institute FishPhone. Send a text to 30644 with the message FISH in all caps, followed by the name of the fish you want to know about, and it'll fire back sustainability info on that species.

Unsettling fact: a farm's farmed fish feces in the water equals the amount of untreated sewage from a town with a population 65,000.

Buy wild fish—even though it may mean a longer food commute—or skip the fish until you're somewhere where they live in the wild.

HOW ALICE'S MAD HATTER GOT HIS NAME

Our playgroup does a monthly Kid's Book Club. At a recent literary session, all the mamas converted to eco-friendly fish-stick zealots when they heard how Alice's Mad Hatter got his name. Open your friends' eyes with this cautionary tale, compliments of Mr. Lewis Carroll. Back in the day, hatters used special felt glue laced with mercury. Enough went "mad" that we now know the term "mad as a hatter." In short, mercury is a known neuro, skin, and reproductive toxin. Want to test your family's mercury levels? For $25 each, Greenpeace will test your hair samples. Go to *www.secureusa.greenpeace.corg/mercury* to learn more.

Quick Tips Down the (Grocery Store) Aisles

Use the following section to help you sort through your local food source options. Whether you're at the farmers' market, CSA, corner store, or grocery, remember to check ingredient labels. Look to see how "high" in the panel an ingredient you want (or don't want) appears. The higher it is, the higher percentage of the product it makes up as an ingredient. One caveat: manufacturers are on to us and may use small quantities of a variety of an unwanted thing in order to make it appear less concentrated. A common example of this is sugar. Look for all kinds of "ose" and "ase" varieties in the label panel that may add up to one whopping big portion of plain old sugar.

If your local life's gotten too busy to visit the store, you may be able to get local produce delivered to your home. Visit *www.farm freshtoyou.com* and *www.spud.com* to find options near you.

Dairy

When it comes to dairy, there's a lot to think about, thanks to the hormones regularly pumped into cows to increase their milk production. The studies on conventional milk processing nearly frightened me enough to swear off dairy or buy our own cow. For starters, the hormone- and antibiotic-laden milk we've chugged for decades seems to correlate with increased early pubescence and decreased fertility rates. From there, health risk claims range from neural damage to cancer. I'm not sure I'll ever have the full facts, but if even a tenth of what's been reported is true, it's worth searching out a certified local dairy or paying the massive premium for organic dairy products.

When buying milk, search for a local dairy certified as antibiotic- and hormone-free or organic. If finding a safe, sustainable dairy source defies your hometown supply, consider switching to goat's milk. Soy, almond, and rice milk are also options.

Once you've found a dairy, buy your milk in plastic or glass gallons (or half gallons if your home consumption means gallons would spoil). These containers use less packaging, and many towns don't yet recycle wax half-gallon containers.

For cheese, it's local or organic again. Buy larger blocks to slice or grate at home. That way there is less packaging, and less energy is used compared to manufacturing pre-cut/grated product.

Stocking up on eggs? Investigate a local co-op. Start at *www .LocalHarvest.org* for a list of egg co-ops and farmers near you. Try your local farmers' market as well. Many produce farmers have eggs as well and will bring them to the next market if you buy in advance. If you're shopping at your local grocery, choosing eggs can be particularly tricky. If you're perplexed by twenty types, go first for organic, then pasture-raised or free-range for drug-free, chilled-out eggs. DHA/omega-rich flavors get bonus points. As always, go for the larger, multidozen packs to reduce packaging.

Grains

Nope, that's not a broken record you hear—local and organic always are best. Buy in whole loaves, or make sure the bread is single bagged if sliced (less packaging). Recycle plastic bags at home.

You've probably heard that breakfast is the most important meal of the day. Therefore, it's especially important to get your cereals right! Purchase your organic cereals and grains in bulk bins and bring your own storage container to cut down on packaging.

Produce

They spray a lot of scary chemicals to keep our fruits and veggies ripe and bug-free for longer periods of time. Buy fresh local, organic, then frozen, then canned. Why is canned so low on the list? It takes ten times the energy to can as to freeze.

You can even freeze your fresh produce at home to use later. Learn how to at *www.clemson.edu*. Visit the site index or the extension programs section. Even I could do it!

When you're buying produce at the store, skip plastic bags to hold fresh fruits and veggies, or bring bags from home. Try Ever-Fresh Green Bags to keep produce fresher, longer. They retail for about $2 a bag (they can be reused up to 10 times) and are available *www .greenbags.com*. Also, skip precut fruits and veggies. These use extra packaging and energy.

Want to prioritize your produce? Here are the top twelve produce items to buy local or organic. If they're not available, skip or buy organic frozen. Go to *www.foodnews.org* to see where other fruits and veggies rank.

1. Nectarines
2. Celery
3. Pears

4. Peaches
5. Apples
6. Cherries
7. Strawberries
8. Grapes
9. Spinach
10. Potatoes
11. Bell Peppers
12. Red Raspberries

GROW YOUR OWN ALTERNATIVES

If growing even a small pot of tomatoes or herbs seems insurmountable, consider joining with neighbors and friends to create a community garden. In addition to making strides toward backyard local life and neighborhood networks, you could make a dent in your community's hunger. Plant a row for the hungry and donate to your local shelter. You may even recruit local shelter residents to help tend the garden. Reap a local feast and richer community in one harvest.

Meat, Poultry, and Fish

As stated earlier, if you really want to improve your carbon footprint as well as your health, buy and eat less meat.

For the times when you simply need a drumstick or a T-bone, buy local, organic chicken and meat if available. If not, buy grassfed or free-range fresh from the butcher. Though these terms do not guarantee that the meats were produced in a sustainable, free-range setting, it's a start.

You can find organic meats via some local livestock ranches. If you're out of luck in your backyard, go online at *www.eatwellguide .org* and *www.maverickranch.com* to find clean beef and poultry.

When you're in the mood for something fishy, buy sustainably fresh-harvested fish. Avoid sodium nitrates in meat and fish products. They can react with your stomach acids to create nitrosamines, which have been identified as carcinogens. Also steer clear of bovine growth hormone (rBGH). These antibiotics go from your meats and dairy into you. Yuck.

Beverages

Read on to learn how Mother Earth (and I) feels about bottled water. Additionally, expand your juices, wines, and beers to include (only) local and organic brands. Look for concentrated versions to wring more juice from the package. Also, choose beverages in glass containers, then paper (even if waxed), or recycled plastic.

Must have a caffeine fix? When you're buying soda, go for fountain soft drinks versus cans. For the stronger stuff, buy local, organic, fair trade coffee and teas.

Household Items

Any mom knows that her grocery list doesn't stop with food items—but you can't let down your guard when it comes to buying household items. Read on for the skinny about nonfood grocery items.

Buy storage and trash bags made from recycled goods (once you've reused every last one you had at home). You can find Seventh Generation brand at most retailers. Glad also has a new recycled line that is available in many stores.

Try to skip disposable plates and cutlery. If you need them, go for the ones made from recycled materials. This is true of all paper products, too. Go to recycled materials for *all* of them (yes, even toilet paper—the recycled version is softer these days). Even better news? Recycled paper products are now available at most local stores for about the same price as nonrecycled goods. Again, look for Seventh Generation, or go to *www.EcoProducts.com* for bulk online buys. When buying your paper goods, choose paper towels and napkins in smaller sheet sizes.

Don't forget Mother Earth when you're having your morning joe, either. Coffee filters now come in reusable hemp or gold filters, so you don't have to use the disposables.

Say No to Bottled Water

All of our local communities are staggeringly parched. For a huge leap in improving your town as well as our world's sustainability, give up bottled water. By now the message has likely reached you, but just in case, consider the fact that 80 percent of the plastic bottles we use never get recycled. Further, bottled water is no healthier for you than tap (in fact, some studies show it's less so) and in most taste tests, subjects can't tell the difference between the local tap water and bottled H2O. So the bottom line when it comes to bottled water is that it isn't better for you, it usually doesn't taste better, it isn't cheap, and it is hard on the environment. It's not only the plastic bottles disrupting Mama Earth. Recent studies cite negative impacts of bringing a natural habitat's water source down in order to fill those one-time gulp bottles up. Stay local and drink from your town tap. Save your money and the world. What a deal.

If you can't imagine giving up the convenience of your bottled water habit, consider your options. Buy a water filter and fill up reusable water bottles from your local tap. You can either install a filter on your sink or use a filter pitcher in your fridge. Many recommend charcoal filters for best results. Some good options are a Brita Filter (available at local hardware stores and at Brita.com) and a More Pure Filter (available at Whole Foods). I installed a More Pure Filter from Whole Foods in my sink at home. It took some professional help, since I tried to install it at the neck of the faucet (no, no, no) instead of the mouth. It worked well, but we unexpectedly tired of an extra gadget taking up sink space and installed a better fridge filter (we donated the sink filter to our local shelter).

Addicted to club soda and seltzer? Try SodaClub's Soda Maker and make your own club! My friend Tish gave one to our friend and club soda connoisseur Crista. She loves it and entertains with soda concoctions day and night. Visit *www.sodaclubusa.com.*

If you don't like any of these options and must have portable water, try BIOTA water in compostable bottles.

Convert Bottles to Cash

Sometimes bottled water can't be skipped because it's too convenient. Parties, large group outings on the road, or too many days (weeks?) behind on cleaning reusable bottles may make bottled water unavoidable. Whatever the reason, scrub a guilty conscience by collecting all the bottles, recycling them for cash (where you can), and donating to your favorite eco-cause.

My local women's community service group, the San Clemente Junior Women's Club, asks members to bring recyclables to our monthly meetings. Women bring enough bags of bottles and cans each month to pack my station wagon out the sunroof. I unload the goods at a local recycling center in exchange for cash to donate back to the group's fundraising efforts. It's an easy way for us to recycle and earn donations to invest in local causes.

You can create your own mass recycling initiative by organizing school or women's organization fundraisers around scooping up these earth-ugly items. Set up either a drop spot or an at-home carpool bottle pickup to convert convenience into local group cash. Now that we have your water covered, let's go over a few sustainable shopping tips.

Sustainable Food Shopping and More

A reminder of one of the most basic, but oft-neglected steps to sustainable shopping: bring your own bags when you shop. We use 10 billion paper bags and 380 billion plastic bags a year. More than 90 percent of these never get recycled. A third end up clogging our water lines and/or choking our animal life.

PRESERVE PARTY

Need another excuse to come together for play? Throw a preserve party. Everyone brings fruits and veggies ready to store for the long haul, as well as reused storage containers. Go beyond simple storage goals and experiment with homemade pesto, applesauce, jams, and fruit butters. Yum. To learn specifics about preserving food, visit the National Home Center for Home Food Preservation at *www.uga.edu/nchfp*. They cover canning, freezing, drying, pickling, and more.

If each of our homes cut out just two plastic bags per week this year, we'd save so many plastic bags that if they were tied together, they would circle the earth 126 times. We already know plastic is toxic, but paper is no better. In many aspects, paper is actually worse because of the trees destroyed and the CO_2 emitted from manufacturing and distributing those bags.

So reuse and recycle the bags you've got and then replace them with reusable bags. Almost every grocery store sells them. For a bit of your signature style, check out *www.reusablebags.com or www.envirosax.com.* If you're always forgetting your bags, try the Envirosax options from emagineGreen.com. Multiple bags easily fit into one. The whole set fits into your palm, your purse, or your car door pocket.

Note: Many local grocery stores now collect bags, but do not actually recycle the bags collected. Play it safe and bring your own bags.

Sustainable Cooking and Storing Tips

You can find a forest of locavore-oriented cookbooks to inspire your eco-conscious cooking. Although no taste-treat recipes appear here, some of my favorite cookbooks incorporating local and sustainable food choices and techniques are:

> *The Sustainable Kitchen Cookbook* by Stu Steins, Judith H.
> Dern and Mary Hinds
> *Holy Cows and Hog Heaven: The Food Buyer's Guide to Farm
> Friendly Food*, by Joel Salatin
> *Food to Live By: The Earthbound Farm Organic Cookbook*,
> by Myra Goodman
> *Super Natural Cooking: Five Ways to Incorporate Whole and
> Natural Foods into Your Cooking*, by Heidi Swanson
> *The Organic Cook's Bible*, by Jeff Cox
> *The Whole Foods Market Cookbook* by Steve Petusevsky

Aside from the actual recipes, you can take many steps to stay sustainable while preparing food. First off, save your local power source by opening the refrigerator and freezer infrequently. Treat each door opening as dollars on your utility bill. Think about what you need, grab it all at once, and wait to clean up until you're ready to put it all back.

Further, make sure that your food is clean and toxin-free. Trim fat off all meats, poultry, and fish. Pesticides and toxins usually collect here (as they also do in dairy fats) . . . yuck. We all know to do it, but make sure you do: wash all your produce—even local and organic—before eating. Save water by washing your fruits and veggies in a bowl. And *don't wash produce until you're ready to eat it or cook it*. Produce has a substance in its skin that helps keep it fresh. Advance washing can accelerate decay and waste your good treats. Store fruits and veggies separately to keep each fresh longer.

When it comes to using your heat sources, use the microwave (takes about one-third as much energy as your stove), then the toaster, then the stovetop, and then the oven. Cover pots and pans during cooking to conserve the heat generated (this also helps to seal in flavors and juices). Don't preheat for cooking times longer than thirty minutes. You won't affect the cooking and you'll save energy. The exception may be baked goods, especially those that require shorter cook times. And, by the same rationale, turn off the oven early—ten minutes before the recommended end of cooking time. Whenever possible, cook in large batches to freeze for later. Cooking uses more energy than freezing.

SAVE TIME, MONEY, AND ENERGY: COOKING CO-OPS

When I moved to Dana Point, I received an invitation to join a cooking co-op. Spearheaded by my friend and fellow locally minded Mama, Kristin K., our cooking co-op specialized in healthy treats and easy eats. Kristin invited five moms to join her in a weekly cooking rotation. She set up the calendar to accommodate family schedules, household taste preferences, and simple preparation and cleanup requirements. We each cooked once every two weeks and received meals twice a week—often savoring the leftovers another night to get four "provided" meals each week. The only downside? My husband discovered I'm not as great a chef as I'd advertised in comparison to co-op partners.

So round up a group of neighbors, sign up for a big bucket of love from your local CSA, and craft a cooking co-op! Gather over an inaugural locally sourced meal and plot your first three months of meals. Feels like a long time period to cover, but you'll be happy you thought through the details and made a commitment to carry you through any start-up hiccups. With a cooking co-op you'll get to know your neighbors better, savor a variety of dinner menus, reap the benefits of bulk buying, save money and—even better—time!

When it comes to the materials for your cookware, deliver on sustainability by opting for cast iron and glass cooking containers. Cast iron lasts a lifetime and adds iron to your diet. Though silicone is also long-lasting and doesn't require additional supplies like aluminum foil or parchment paper, many nonstick finishes contain a likely carcinogen (PFOA). Also, silicone often ends up in landfills instead of recycling plants. Visit *www.pyrex.com* or *www.bedbathandbeyond .com* for good options. Try stainless steel cookie sheets—you may need to use parchment paper or olive oil to keep cookies from sticking to the pan, but you'll be avoiding possible carcinogens. You'll find good choices at *www.cookwareessentials.com* and *www.target.com.*

Now, what to do with all those leftovers? Store them in glass containers—Anchor Hocking makes great stacking store-and-reheat containers—which are available at Target and most grocery stores. As mentioned earlier, never heat food in plastic containers—studies show that chemicals from plastic leak into the food.

Finally, use parchment paper and aluminum foil instead of plastic wrap. They're more easily recycled, and you can use parchment paper in the microwave. If you must use plastic wrap, know that Glad Cling Wrap, Handi-Wrap, and Saran Wrap are at least PVC-free.

Sustainable Cleanup

Two rules of thumb for cleaning up after your good local meal: use less water, and use eco-friendly cleaners.

My first piece of advice is really a lovely tip: skip prerinsing your dishes—put them straight into the dishwasher and save water. Most dishwashers can handle it. If yours can't, try controlling the water used by filling up a tub with water and prewashing everything at once. If you've been pondering upgrading your dishwasher, and going for the long term gives you the perfect excuse, check out Energy Star appliances.

Also try reducing sink faucet water pressure. Either use the handle at half-mast or install a flow reducer (check out Energy Star or WaterSense brands). We tried one for our kitchen and are happy campers. We also installed them in our bathroom sinks (more on that in Chapter 6).

Don't run the water to get it hot. If you really need hot water right out the gate, install a tankless heater under the sinks where you need immediate heat. (The master bath may be another place you need this. See Chapter 6 for information about the heater we use.)

Try using homemade or earth-friendly cleaners. Look for phosphate-free products as well as bigger packages made from recycled materials and refillable pump dispenser options. Most retailers now carry eco-brands like Method, Planet Earth, and Seventh Generation.

Local, Sustainable Dining and Takeout

When you're ready to vacate the kitchen and give the dishwasher a rest, you can still stay true to your local life goals. Using the following resources to find restaurants that cook with local, organic, and free trade ingredients. And, if you're in a new town or can't find a tasty locally owned eatery, you can try a few national chains, such as Chipotle (clean meats and local produce) and—perhaps surprisingly— TGIF (antibiotic-free meats), that are working to incorporate local and sustainable practices in each location.

To find local restaurants near you, check out:

www.Eatwellguide.org
www.locallectual.com
www.Naturalfoodnet.com/nfnportal/COFDSearch.aspx
www.Dinegreen.com

Keep a few sustainability tips in mind when ordering takeout:

- Request no napkins or cutlery when you phone in your order.
- Request no Styrofoam. Even if it isn't currently possible for a restaurant to package your food without Styrofoam, if enough folks hear the request, we may see some changes.
- Skip the drive-through. Studies show it's not any faster, and you're spewing carbon dioxide emissions as you wait. Burn calories instead of carbon gases—turn off the car and go inside.

It's tough to control what goes into what you eat when you're eating out. Still, you can target local restaurants serving locally produced ingredients. And, to contribute to the earth's longevity, try to under-order. If you're anything like my husband and me, you order about twice as much as you need because it all sounds good. Although you can (and absolutely MUST) take it home with you to relive a great night, save the inbound energy required to make those portions in the first place. Order half of what you think you want. If you're still hungry after finishing, you can always order again.

Finally, remember that 100 percent adherence is an unnecessarily high hurdle to set. Follow a few local sourcing guidelines. Start by choosing just ten items from your grocery list to shift to a local source. Look for locally made and organically grown goods. Then move onto locally processed goods. Next choose local businesses to support. If no local business option exists, opt for sustainably sourced and processed products. Last, look for products "of the earth" or "taste of the earth" (*terroir*), which opens up food items from regions with a focused specialty, such as Parmesan cheese from Parma. Over time, you'll diversify your food choices and build your local economy. A double taste treat, indeed.

Spotlight: GrowingGreat Founder Marika Bergsund

Marika Bergsund has been an advocate of slow food and local living since her school days racing sailboats and hiking California's trails. After graduating from Boalt Hall School of Law, Marika practiced environmental law and went on to coauthor a leading book series on California and federal environmental law (find Dwyer & Bergsund's *California Environmental Laws Annotated* and Dwyer & Bergsund's *Federal Environmental Laws Annotated* at *www.west.thomson.com*). As a mother of three, Marika wanted to build a sense of community awareness and healthy lifestyle choices for her family. She began by gardening at home and teaching her kids how to grow and cook with fresh fruits and vegetables. Marika found that the more hands-on they were, the more produce they polished off their plates (a secret for all moms yearning to get more veggies into kids' bellies).

As fresh as Marika's food was at home, she still battled school menus and their often less-than-ideal food choices. Marika decided to tackle two issues at once: improve kids' food options and help more children learn about the benefits of growing foods and making healthy food decisions. In 1999, Marika started the GrowingGreat garden and education program in her children's elementary school. GrowingGreat now serves twenty-one schools, reaching 28,000 children and adults annually and providing a template for schools across the nation that are working to amp up children's connection to the land and smart nutrition.

What is GrowingGreat?

GrowingGreat is a nonprofit garden and nutrition education organization dedicated to inspiring children and adults to adopt healthy eating habits. Since 1999, we have been offering comprehensive nutrition education and school garden programs to elementary school students, their families, and community partners. Our School Garden

Program teaches schools how to start and maintain a garden as well as provides grade-specific garden lessons. Our Classroom Nutrition Programs educate children about how to make healthy food choices and to cook and eat nutritious menus. We bring the farm to the school through our Harvest of the Month programs with local farmers' markets. We also host community events that promote community awareness, healthy eating, and sustainable lifestyles.

What led you to start GrowingGreat?

Making smarter long-term decisions to take care of our world—and ourselves—has always been a priority. I saw how much more engaged my kids became in caring about "earth-friendly" issues and good eating choices when they had their hands directly in our garden. Many of my friends were wrestling with similar issues in raising children, so it seemed developing an in-school program could help involve kids at an early enough age to impact their lifelong thinking. Creating a garden, tending to the fruits and veggies, harvesting the crops, and then cooking with the produce fosters a deeper appreciation for the environment.

How can interested moms either get GrowingGreat on their children's campus or start a similar program in their school system?

We offer a lot of information on our website about adopting our garden and nutrition programs. Moms could visit *www.growing great.typepad.com/growinggreat* to learn more or to contact us.

For general information on gardening with your kids, go to *www .kidsgardening.com* for a wide variety of resources, from suggested planting plans and tips to kid-friendly gardening tools to purchase. The California School Garden Network, *www.csgn.org*, has a wealth of info on school gardens for California and beyond. Check out *www.myhealthyschool.com* to learn how to make your home and your children's school healthier and more eco-friendly. You can find GrowingGreat's intro to school gardens article and sample lessons in their gardening section. Other important topics on the site are healthy school lunches, waste reduction and recycling at schools, and "greening your campus." For information on protecting your children from environmental risks, go to *www.healthychild.org.*

What are some of your favorite tips for moms trying to create an eco-friendly home and environmentally aware family?

My top two tips are 1) *Lead by Example* and 2) *Make Family Dinners a Habit.* Leading by example means making sure that you take care of your own health by eating right, exercising, and protecting the environment. Our children watch our every move for guidance on how to live their lives. When we celebrate eating a delicious piece of fresh fruit for snack, drink a big glass of water, or pick up trash we find on the ground, we are teaching far more powerful lessons than could ever be learned from books or lectures. And the family dinner table is ground zero for teaching both healthy eating and your family's values. A family that sits and eats (and even better, cooks) together enjoys both the love and health that come from sharing a family meal and also has a regular opportunity to discuss their lives, interests, and family priorities.

"Tell me what you eat, I'll tell you who you are."

—Anthelme Brillat-Savarin

4

SUSTAINING YOUR BEAUTY
AND MAMA EARTH

> "I'm tired of all this nonsense about beauty being only skin-deep. That's deep enough. What do you want, an adorable pancreas?"
>
> —Jean Kerr

Now that you've anchored your local life compass via your true (inner) beauty, let's dive into some of the more superficial but fun elements of your personal care: lotions and potions. Since your skin absorbs—and in effect digests—60 percent (yes, 6-0!) of what you put on it, bathroom cabinets add a whole new shelf to the "you are what you eat" life mantra.

EYE OPENERS
- We absorb 60 percent of what's *on* our skin, *into* our skin— almost five pounds of man-made chemicals each year.
- We ingest four pounds of lipstick in a lifetime.
- More than 80 percent of 900+ sunscreens deliver inadequate protection and often don't meet product claims.

THE LOCAL LIFE GUIDELINES FOR PERSONAL CARE
1. Shop local and extend the life of your personal care treasures.
2. Buy local and organic ingredients—the more the better.

3. Know what's in your bottles and jars: Use Safecosmetics.org, Cosmeticsdatabase.com, Lesstoxicguide.ca, and Ewg.org. All are good product databases rich with information on your personal care products.

4. Choose products free of animal testing: We can look good without rat and rabbit testing, yes?

5. Shed packaging: Opt for glass and paper versus plastic; try concentrates; buy in bulk with refillable pumps. And skip disposable products—especially razors.

The Sustainability Screen: Personal Care

Change the World

1. Start Here!

Know the fifteen ingredients to avoid

Buy products with less packaging

Choose eco-friendly, nontoxic sunscreen

Hold your own products party

3. Reach For It!

Make your own products

Shorten and cool down family showers

Screen brands and stores by CSC compact, USDA Organic seal, animal-free testing

IMPACT

2. Why Not?

Buy more concentrated versions of your favorite products

Avoid aluminum in antiperspirants

Eliminate disposable razors

Use products made from recycled products

4. Save for Last!

Skip the makeup if you can

Skip the perfume

Skip the lotions

Make your own soap from bar scraps

Baby Steps Count

Simple   **EASE TO DO**   Disruptive

6. Use less water: Take shorter showers (if lusciously locked Jennifer Anniston can do it, so can we); brush your teeth and wash your face with the tap turned off. *Think: Turning off the faucet for one minute saves four gallons of water.*

Where to Get the Good Stuff

Your cleanest bet will be homegrown goods. Try a Mama Mix Party or check out *www.Eco-Me.com* for starter kits to sample a myriad of homemade magic potions and lotions.

Mama Mix Party

My mom is the Mother of All Mama Magic Mixes. She whips up homemade skin care products, cosmetics, and perfumes with the tiniest wiggle of her wrinkle-free nose. She makes "beauty cooking" fun, creative, and effective—so much so I don't even notice the frugal element of making my own delights.

However, sometimes mixing your own goods results in a lot of waste as you learn your favorite recipes and make too big a batch for one face. Throw an at-home Mama Mix Spa party where you can mix a variety of beauty batches to sample amongst friends. Poll attendees a few days prior to find out what everyone's beauty wishes are, and make a master list of ingredients in advance. Visit your farmers' markets and co-ops to supply the raw materials. Then, spice up the evening with a locavore potluck and neighborhood winery samples.

As the magic unfolds, collect samples of favorites and send everyone home with jars (reused jam, mustard, or even mayonnaise jars, please) full of the evening's favorites potions as well as a commitment to compare notes within sixty days to find the winners. For some of the best recipes, check out *www.realsimple.com*, *www.about.com*, *www.mothernature.com*, and *www.goherbalremedies.com*. Or try the book *The Green Beauty Guide: Your Essential Resource to Organic and Natural Skin Care, Hair Care, Makeup, and Fragrances,* by Julie Gabriel.

No time to cook your own? Shop the following brands and stores for products that maintain your fountain of youth as well as Mama Earth's. Though not every product in every brand or store will be 100 percent local, organic, and sustainable, these companies do offer a broad selection of great products with mostly organic ingredients and environmentally friendly practices.

Remember, you make the market. Keep demanding local, organic, and eco-friendly products, and more will come.

Linsly's Picks for Sustainable Sustenance

Screening for products made with ingredients and processes that love the earth as much as my face, I found a few favorites. I adore Aubrey, Evan Healy, Pangea skin/body care, and Zia for everything. Play around with those and you should be a happy girl. Want more specifics? Details follow. Look for the 🏷 sign for value options.

For Your Lovely Face

Let's start with the basics. (🏷) Zia, Evan Healy, and Pangea all make affordable, good-to-you-and-the-earth cleansing and exfoliating lines. Splurge on Stella McCartney's CARE eco-line. Delicious! For moisturizers, add in the Nature's Gate (🏷) line and Alba's higher-end Cerenade label. And, for those giggling, grinning, expressing-all-things, full-of-life lil' creases dancing from your eyes, turn to Pangea and Aubrey eye creams.

When you need to work overtime on your face's overwork, rest easy with Lavera's luscious anti-aging line, Stella's CARE Vitamin C aid, and Anne Marie Borling's masks. A worthwhile investment? The Essence—fully organic—spa line. The trusty Evan Healy, Pangea, and Zia also offer rescue treatments at a good price. Finding yourself bafflingly blessed with both a few lines and a few . . . bumps? Try Desert Essence's acne treatment.

When you're ready to accent nature's work of art, try ZuZu, Lavera, and Dr. Hauschka for good foundation, powder, and blush lines. They don't streak, don't cake, and do . . . enhance. Look for wood-based pencils versus plastic for eye and lip lines. I like Gabriel pencils and ZuZu liquid eye color lines. Lavera makes my favorite mascara. If only I had my three-year-old's two-inch-long eyelashes. Sigh.

SECRET GARDEN FOR YOUR LOTIONS AND POTIONS

A fabulous resource for you beauties is the Cosmetics Database (*www.cosmeticsdatabase.com*). They've done the homework on thousands of products so you can find your favorites and assess the risks.

Throw a sample party with your Mama friends. All you need is your favorite products, samples of what may become favorites, one Internet connection, and feast treats. Sprawl in front of a fireplace and trade recommendations while looking up how your tried-and-true stack up against the Campaign for Safe Cosmetics (CSC) and Environmental Working Group (EWG) sustainability screen (*www.cosmeticsdatabase.com*). As you sift to find group favorites, consider bulk buys. Manufacturers often offer group discounts when you team up for a bigger quantity.

Experiment with what you have, and then set up a Girls' Night Out with an eco-makeover pre-party to trial run the best of the bets.

To keep the lead out—literally—stick to organic lipstick lines. My personal favorites are Hemp Organics, Zia, and Essence (available at local spas). For lip balms, go back to Pangea and Alba (an especially yummy one). And, to accent your shimmering smile, you can keep your teeth white, your breath fresh, and Mama Earth smiling with Kiss My Face toothpaste. It tastes the best of all the local, organic, and natural options. Both Recycline and Preserve make excellent toothbrushes and tongue scrapers from recycled plastics.

UVA vs. UVB vs. What U. C.

Although it may be tough to find locally made sunscreens that truly protect you and sustain the earth, it's worth knowing what you're looking for, should you come across a good local source. Start by understanding what protection you really need (most likely all of it), and then learn which ingredients deliver that protection with the lightest earth impact. Radiation, skin damage, skin cancer, and aging come mostly from UVA rays. Sunburn comes mostly from UVB rays.

The real damage? Many sunscreens we buy don't guard against what they claim, and even many that do seep toxins into our skin and environment. What's an outdoor-enjoying-Mama-Earth-loving girl to do? Recognize that the FDA only regulates sunscreen to protect against sunburn—UVB rays. Again, know your ingredients—check the cosmetics database (*www.cosmeticsdatabase.com*) for ingredient details on products you have and to ensure you've *also* got UVA protection.

Another reason to review the cosmetics database: The Environmental Working Group (*www.ewg.org*) researched 900 products and found that most did not do what they claimed—one in eight of the highest SPF level products didn't protect against any UVA rays. The study also found claims such as "all day protection," "stays on in water," and "blocks all harmful rays" aren't true and fail on the FDA's current draft sunscreen regulations. A quick online check will tell if what you've got is what you need.

When perusing the ingredients panel, watch for Parsol 1789. It's been linked to liver damage, Parkinson's disease, and some cancers. Some studies have found that four ingredients (parabens, cinnamate, benzophenone, and a camphor derivative) commonly found in sunscreens wash off into the water—and damage the water world by bleaching and killing what grows below. Titanium dioxide sunscreens may be a better option; however, there are some questions on those as well. Since titanium dioxide and zinc oxide often come from ingredients classified as nano-scale, some scientists have raised questions about toxicity.

A work-around? The European Union has ingredients with more effective UVA filters, but the FDA has not yet approved these products in the United States. There are some winners now available closer to home:

OPTIONS AVAILABLE IN THE U.S. INCLUDE:

- California Baby Sunscreen: *www.californiababy.com*
- Green People: *www.greenpeople.co.uk*
- Weleda: *www.weleda.co.uk*
- Dr. Hauschka: *www.drhauschka.com*
- Yaoh: *www.yaoh.co.uk*
- Neal's Yard: *www.nealsyardremedies.com*
- Aubrey Organics: *www.aubrey-organics.com*

For Your Crown

In addition to providing shine, body, and bounce, I like hair care lines to help me smell yummy. How else can I hope to cover up the scent of crushed bunny crackers, this morning's Mocha, and my littlest one's—um—leftover milk? Sweet-smelling and sustainable stuff is hard to come by (see page 81 for the stinky details on artificial fragrances), but the following lines offer a helping hand. For shampoo, conditioner, deep care treatments, and styling products, try the John Masters, EO, Desert Essence, Kiss My Face, and J/A/S/O/N lines. I especially like the Desert Essence raspberry shampoo and EO's lavender conditioner.

Body

A deep soak in the bathtub is too rare a treat. Simulate blessed escape with luxurious body lotions, soaps, and shaving gels. One sniff of Lush soaps and soaks takes me to a virtual spa bathtub. Dr. Brommers offers a bit of antiquity and humor in their soaps (which can also double as safe, effective home cleaning products). Pangea and Origins (Organic Line) lotions soften without feeling greasy. Blooming Lotus and Trillium make soothing exfoliants. Turn to Tracie Martyn's SkinCare Shakti line for firming cream, and Pacific Shaving for decadent shaving gels.

Time for some heavier maintenance? Sugar instead of wax (which has petrochemicals) with Ancient Egyptian Art of Body Sugar. Being good and steering clear of suntans? Look for "plant-derived DHA" in body or face bronzer ingredients list, concentrated at 2 to 5 percent. Try Recycline again for razors or a great sharpener product called the Razor Saver. Last, go for chlorine-free, organic cotton on all sanitary products. Try NatraCare and Lunapads brands.

For Your Touch

Softening and anti-aging products come via the lotions mentioned in the previous section. However, sustainable nail care can be a bit trickier. Steer clear of alcohol- or solvent-based lines (which unfortunately means most mass-market lines). Try water-based products such as Honeybee Gardens or Delore NailCare. Also look for real cotton balls versus synthetic, which take 70 percent more energy to make.

For Your Little Delights

Fortunately, good, organic kids' care lines have become much more affordable and accessible. My personal favorite is California Baby ( ). Other solid lines are Clean Well (especially hand sanitizer), Earth Mama Angel Baby Organics, Little Sprout ( ), and

Terressentials. For eco-diaper options, see The Stinky Facts about Diapers later in this chapter.

For Your Hero

Dressing up The Mr. is always good fun. Two winners on price and quality are Herban Cowboy (how can you not love this line?) and Living Nature. Pacific Shaving also keeps him soft and smooth. Try Dr. Alkaitis and Dr. Hauschka for good men's skin-care lines.

The Nitty Gritty: The Gory Details of Beauty Products

It's easy to look good and care for your community as well. Between the proliferation of farmers' markets and co-ops and local products finding their way to national chain-store shelves, there are enough local and sustainable personal care brands to make your clean-conscience glamour effortless. If what you find in stores doesn't please you, look online. You'll find endless homemade recipes and luxurious concoctions online. And Internet shopping options grow daily. Your challenge will be in selecting the shades, flavors, and scents you relish. The local and sustainable parts can be simple.

Finding locally made beauty products may baffle at first. But, as with food, many farmers' markets and co-ops offer excellent selections of locally made glamour gear. If you're striking out there, a number of online search directories can help you mine your community for lovely things. Try these:

www.locallectual.com: The site lists recommendations by product categories. Search by product, retailer and/or Zip Code.
www.local.com: A more generic search engine, it screens recommendations by Zip Code. You can further filter the results by sustainability criteria.

Coming back to a primary sustainability guideline, extend the life of the beauty treasures you already have. Keep them dry, out of the sun, and as clean as possible.

Stay Local and Organic

Ladies, the standard recipe in our cosmetics frightens. Solution: Know your ingredients and demand local, organic, animal-friendly elements in your products. Just as in food production, local and organic production practices for personal care products mean fewer pesticides, toxins, and waste on the planet. Remember my brain surgeon dinner companion? He said everything you put in and on your body should be organic. Like many experts, he was highlighting the reality that you ingest almost as much through your skin as you do through your stomach. By choosing local and organic ingredients, you do well by Mother Earth while doing your best with what she gave you.

Here's a stunner: Of the 10,500 ingredients the FDA has identified as used in U.S. personal care products, close to 90 percent have not been evaluated for safety by the Cosmetic Ingredient Review (CIR), the FDA, or any other publicly accountable institution.

But, how do we know which ingredients and which products to choose as we shop our local sources?

Know what's in your bottles and jars (refer back to Secret Garden for Your Lotions and Potions earlier in this chapter for resources). Conventional health and beauty products include industrial chemicals as basic ingredients. Many U.S. personal care products contain carcinogens, pesticides, reproductive toxins, endocrine disruptors, plasticizers, degreasers, and surfactants.

YOUR "STEER CLEAR" LIST: THE FRIGHTENING 15

1. Parabens
2. Phthalates (DBP and DEHP are most toxic)

3. Isopropyl alcohol
4. By-products of crude oil: mineral oil, paraffin, coal tar, petroleum
5. Mercury
6. PEG (polyethylene glycol)—a petroleum derivative
7. PG (propylene glycol)
8. Sodium lauryl sulfate (SLS) and sodium laureth sulfate (SLES)
9. DEA (diethanolamine), MEA (monoethanolamine), and TEA (triethanolamine)
10. Color: synthetics marked as FD&C or D&C pigments
11. Synthetic fragrances (The Scent of a Toxin . . .)
12. Imidazolidinyl urea and DMDM hydantoin
13. Lead acetate
14. Chlorine: used in sanitary products; creates dioxin (a known carcinogen) as a byproduct.
15. Titanium dioxide: the jury's still out on this one

If the chemistry in your cosmetics furrows your already-furrowed-more-than-you'd-like brow, review Linsly's Picks for Sustainable Sustenance for manufacturers and retailers who'll get you the good stuff. However, for detail on what these ingredients are, how they're used, why to avoid them, and how to spot them in your products, flip to page 74.

Rise Above Animal Testing

How sustainable can a product be if it required testing on rabbits and rats? Aside from the seemingly absurd assertion that we should test products on animals in order to make humans look better, it's just not so nice. Best certification labels to trust are Bunny Label and PETA. The organizations behind these labels review and certify products based on adherence to animal-friendly practices.

Shed Packaging

Go for glass and paper packages before plastic and look for post-consumer recycled materials (you'll spot the circular arrow seal or copy that calls it out).

Choose refillable cosmetics—eye shadows, blushers, powders, foundations. Use refillable pumps. (A true story: my husband still uses a refillable shampoo pump dispenser he bought four years ago. Admittedly the other kind of green first motivated him, but now he's eco-friendly too.) Add in bulk sizes and concentrates to stretch the original packaging.

Opt for solids (soaps/washes) over liquids. And double up with two-in-one products (for example, shampoo and conditioner).

Try to skip cosmetics sold in plastic containers. The plastics are made from nonrenewable fossil fuels. Usually, these containers aren't recycled and go straight to your community landfill. Many recyclers refuse molded plastic containers, such as compacts or plastic jars. Even when manufacturers claim the packaging is recyclable (because it's made from a recyclable plastic resin, such as #1 PET), recycling programs say no due to the shape of the container or the fact that the plastic resin is not noted directly on the packaging. Also make a promise to give up disposable razors. Really, we all know disposable and sustainable do not go together.

Use Less Water

It's tough to live a sustainable life if we waste one of our most precious and threatened resources: water. We tend to dress, gloss, and sass amidst gallons of water. Here are some ways to cut water use back (or off):

- Install sink faucet water-pressure reducers. Try WaterSense products, available at Home Depot and Lowe's.

- Worth a quick repeat: shorten showers. Impossible? No. Noticeable? Maybe. While you're at it, try cooling them down a bit and installing a low-flow showerhead. Try Evolve Shower Heads, found at Home Depot or Lowe's. You still get good water pressure.
- Stop running the water to get it hot. Bring the heat to your sink or shower via mini-tankless water heaters. Try PowerStar, available at Lowe's or Home Depot.

The Stinky Facts about Diapers

Eye-opener: The average baby goes through 5,000 diapers before being potty-trained. Since disposable diapers make up 95 percent of diaper changes, we're clogging up landfills at an alarming rate. What's a good solution for your wee ones' poops right now? The diaper debate is almost as famous as "paper or plastic," and just as circular. Disposable diapers don't biodegrade, they stack up in landfills, and are often made with plastic or other chemical toxins. Cloth diapers erase immediate landfill concerns, but use energy to wash and—depending on your detergent—emit toxins in our waterways. Plus, the hassle of cloth diapers often makes them impractical. Fortunately, a few more eco-friendly options are now available.

Hybrid diapers: Diapers such as gDiapers offer an optimal solution: the convenience of disposable diapers with the reusability of cloth. These diapers use a cloth wrap combined with a biodegradable and flushable disposable insert. Ideally, you flush the insert, but in a bind, you can throw it away knowing it's biodegradable. One downside is that the outer cloth wrap cannot be sized as your baby grows, so you need to buy new, larger ones, just as you would for disposable diapers.

Disposable with shades of green: When disposable, store-bought diapers are what you need to have, shop for low-impact diapers: chlorine-free, made with easy-on-the-earth materials, and gel-free if possible. Available brands include Earth's Best, Nature Baby Care, Seventh Generation, Tender Care, and Tushies (gel-free).

Cloth diapers: If cloth diapers suit your style, a few brands receive high marks for absorbency, comfort, and durability. Try BooBear Buns (made from hemp, which means they're a bit thinner), Bum Genius, Happy Heinys, and FuzziBunz.

And next time you're in Ireland (which almost counts as local for our extended Donnelly clan), check out the leading compostable diaper, EcoBaby. To date, they don't ship outside of the magic Island—which is probably a good thing, since flying compostable diapers to the United States would seem to negate the sustainability benefit.

Overwhelmed? You can skip (or at least minimize) the whole thing by trying infant potty training. Infant potty training advocates maintain that babies have a window of receptivity to potty training cues between four and five months. They cite other cultures and pre-diaper times as evidence of babies' ability to potty train. Feeling brave? See BabyParenting.about.com, Timl.com, or *The Infant Potty Training Book* by Laurie Boucke for more details.

🏷 Visit *www.diapers.com* for bulk buying and regular coupons.

The Frightening Fifteen

Okay—take a deep breath—and welcome to CosmeticsChem 101. It's worth revisiting your college science days in order to learn how to better screen anything you come across on your local sourcing quest. These ingredients erode our world—and too often, our bodies and skin as well.

Parabens

Parabens are chemical compounds used to preserve food as well as pharmaceutical and personal care products. They extend a product's shelf life.

Parabens are absorbed through your skin (as well as gastrointestinal tract and blood, but you're not likely eating your cosmetics). They alter hormone levels and are linked to cancer, infertility, and impaired fetal development.

You can find parabens in most personal care products: shampoos, moisturizers, lipsticks, lip balms, mascaras, shaving gels, cleansing gels, toothpaste, and personal lubricants.

You can spot parabens by keeping a close eye on your ingredient list. Watch out for methylparaben, ethylparaben, propylparaben, or butylparaben.

Phthalates

Phthalates make plastics more flexible and bind things like fragrance and color to personal care products.

They are considered hazardous waste and are regulated as air and water pollutants, but are not regulated for things we put on our skin and hair. DBP and DEHP are the most toxic. Phthalates are linked to birth defects, reproductive harm and infertility (female and male), cancer, early puberty onset, organ toxicity, and neuron toxicity.

Many categories have phthalates because they add scent and color. The most common product categories are toys, sunblock, nail polish, deodorant, and hair care. Phthalates don't show up on labels because the chemicals are an ingredient in the fragrance or color. A trade secret loophole in labeling laws enables companies to exclude fragrance ingredients. However, since it's a primary ingredient when present in most nail polish and removers, you should see "phthalates" in the ingredients for those products.

Phthalates go by names such as:

- 1,2-Benzenedicarboxylic Acid, Dibutyl
- Ester; Dibutyl 1,2-Benzenedicarboxylate; Dibutyl
- Ester 1,2-Benzenedicarboxylic Acid; DBP; Dibutyl
- Phthalate; Dibutyl Phthalate; Dibutyl Phthalates; DI-N-
- Butylphthalate, 1,2-Benzenedicarboxylic Acid, Diethyl
- Ester; Diethyl Diethylphthalate.

Isopropyl Alcohol

Isopropyl alcohol is aliphatic alcohol (also used in antifreeze and shellac), a flammable, colorless liquid that often smells like alcohol. Isopropyl alcohol basically helps change the natural properties of other ingredients. It's a fragrance ingredient, solvent, and antifoaming and viscosity-decreasing agent.

Isopropyl alcohol is a poisonous substance linked to neurological disorders and often irritates eyes and skin.

Isopropyl alcohol is found in shampoo, lotions, mouthwash, nail polish, astringents, many makeup products, and perfumes. You can spot isopropyl alcohol by keeping an eye out for the following ingredients:

- Butanol
- Ethanol (antibacterial agent)
- Isopropanol,
- Methanol, Isopropyl Alcohol, 2-Hydroxypropane
- Methylethanol
- 2-Propanol
- Sec-Propyl Alcohol

- 2Propanol
- Propan-2-OL

By-products of Crude Oil

Petroleum derivatives coat the skin to lock in moisture and seem to moisturize as well as prevent drying and chafing. By-products of crude oil include mineral oil, paraffin, coal tar, and petroleum.

So why steer clear of these rude and crude by-products? Well, there's the disturbing idea that you're putting the same base ingredients on your children's face that you put in your gas tank. The toxins, carcinogens, and environmental angst over fossil fuel products are the same whether it's black goop or sweet-smelling lotion. Plus, the stuff clogs your pores, making it tough for your body to get rid of the toxins it already has. These lovely little oil wells show up as things like acne and rashes. Sexy. And, since these substances smother the skin, they keep oxygen out and actually dry out your skin. This, in turn, slows down normal cell development and results in premature aging—the opposite of your fervent hope and prayer.

Many items contain these no-do-gooders, but the most likely offenders are moisturizers, diaper creams, foundations, lipsticks and lip balms, hair relaxers, shampoos, dandruff/scalp treatments, anti-aging creams, perfumes, mascara, anti-itch/rash creams, bath oils, and salt soaks. Fortunately, you can call these like you see 'em: if you see mineral oil, paraffin, coal tar, tar, or petroleum on your ingredient list, run.

Mercury

In personal care products, mercury or mercury-based compounds act as a preservative, extending shelf life. Remember the Mad Hatter anecdote? Skip the neuro, skin, and reproductive toxin. You can find mercury in mascara (mostly cake based, such as Paula Dorf and La Femme), eye drops, ointment, and deodorants.

Look for thimerosal, mercury, mer, thiol, or HG (all code words for mercury) on ingredient labels.

PEG

PEG (polyethylene glycol, a petroleum derivative) shows up in many cleansers because it dissolves oils and grease.

Unfortunately, it cleans a little too well. PEG strips off natural protective oils and puts the immune system at risk.

In addition, PEG, PG, and other petroleum derivatives contain an impurity known as 1,4-dioxane. 1,4-dioxane's primary use is as a manufacturing solvent or fumigant. It also makes great bubbles. 1,4-dioxane is a known carcinogen as well as a skin and lung irritant. It's suspected to be a kidney and nervous system toxin. And, since it bubbles and sudses so well, you may get multiple doses a day. You can find PEG in cleansers, deodorants, shampoos, toothpastes, and mouthwash. Keep an eye out for the following ingredients:

- PEG
- polyethylene
- polyethylene glycol
- polyoxyethylene
- "-eth-" products such as sodium laureth sulfate, ceteareth, or oleth
- oxynol

Propylene Glycol (PG)

Propylene glycol (PG) is a surfactant and carries moisture in cosmetics. PG is the active ingredient in antifreeze; the EPA requires workers using the substance to wear gloves and avoid skin contact.

As an added bonus, you may get our bubbly friend — 1,4-dioxane — as an impurity / by-product of Propylene Glycol.

Research has linked propylene glycol to brain, kidney, and liver abnormalities. If you accidentally swig some, add respiratory irritation and nausea to the benefits list. This unfriendly ingredient is found in moisturizers, hair color and bleaches, anti-aging crèmes, cleansers, conditioner, styling gel/lotion, shampoos, body wash/cleanser, and sunscreen. Keep an eye out for PG and propylene glycol listed on the ingredient panel of your products.

Sodium Lauryl Sulfate (SLS) and Sodium Laureth Sulfate (SLES)

SLS and SLES are relatives of sulphuric acid. Because they are detergents, sudsers, and surfactants (which means they make products easier to apply and foamier), they show up most often in soap, shampoos, and toothpaste. Not only can they damage the immune system and irritate the skin, but once your skin absorbs it, SLS also mimics the hormone estrogen. Researchers have cited this as a factor in male infertility, breast cancer, and menopausal issues. Last, dioxane often contaminates SLS and SLES as well.

SLS and SLES are most often found in soaps/washes, shampoos, bubble-baths, toothpaste, shaving cream, mascara, mouthwash, moisturizer, and sunblocks. They often go by the pseudonyms of sodium lauryl sulfate and sulfuric acid monododecyl ester sodium salt. Some products dressed up as "natural" list SLS with the phrase "derived from coconut."

DEA, MEA, and TEA

DEA (diethanolamine), MEA (monoethanolamine), and TEA (triethanolamine) are fragrance ingredients, pH adjusters, surfactants, and emulsifying agents. They enhance other foaming agents.

They also disrupt hormones, can potentially cause cancer, and often trigger allergies. DEA is easily absorbed through the skin, and accumulates in body organs, even the brain. It's been shown to damage the liver, kidney, brain, spinal cord, bone marrow, and skin.

Moisturizer, anti-aging creams, sunscreen SPF 15 and above, facial cleanser, mascara, styling gel/lotion, foundation, shaving cream, and eye creams can all contain DEA, MEA, and TEA. Look for the following ingredients in your products:

- DEA (diethanolamine)
- MEA (monoethanolamine)
- TEA (triethanolamine)
- Cocamide DEA or MEA
- DEA-cetyl phosphate
- DEA oleth-3 phosphate
- Myristamide DEA
- Stearamide MEA
- Lauramide DEA
- Linoleamide MEA
- Oleamide DEA
- TEA-lauryl sulfate

Synthetic Colors

Synthetic colors such as FD&C or D&C pigments usually come from coal and petroleum. They add longer-lasting color than do natural color dyes. Food manufacturers use the same products to spice up our food's eye-candy appeal. Many of these colors are considered carcinogenic. Some block oxygen absorption. Unfortunately, they can be found in almost all personal care products. Luckily, they're easy to spot on your ingredient lists. They show up as FD&C or D&C, followed by a color, and then a number. For example: FD&C Red 21.

Synthetic Fragrances

Who knew that something that makes our products—and us—smell so good could be so bad for us? These sweet-smellers often contain carcinogens that also cause nervous system toxicity, allergies, and mental challenges, including depression, hyperactivity, and irritability. Scarily, they're found in most categories of personal care products—any product with scent.

These are especially hard to sniff out, too. As is the case for phthalates, manufacturers only have to list the word "fragrance." So unless a fragrance is called out as an essential oil or as certified organic, pass.

Imidazolidinyl Urea and DMDM Hydantoin

Imidazolidinyl urea and DMDM hydantoin are preservatives. While their main goal is to extend shelf life, they're not good for *your* life. They release formaldehyde, a carcinogen, into your body. Because they release formaldehyde, they can also cause a myriad of issues in your respiratory, heart, and nervous systems. These issues often manifest as dizziness, joint pain, chronic fatigue, asthma, and/or coughing. Plus, if not synthetic, urea comes from, ummm . . . animal pee.

Imidazolidinyl urea and DMDM hydantoin show up in moisturizer, anti-aging creams, facial cleanser, eye shadow, powder, mascara, sunscreen SPF 15, body wash/cleanser, and around-the-eye cream. Keep an eye on your ingredient panel to make sure neither is listed.

Lead Acetate

Lead acetates are color additives most often used in hair coloring products and cleansers. Unfortunately, lead acetate also is a known reproductive and developmental toxin. The good news here, if there is any: Products containing lead acetates must carry a warning label. It usually reads something like "Caution: Contains lead acetate. For external use only."

Chlorine

In personal care products, chlorine makes things white and bright. It's dangerous because it releases the carcinogen discussed above, Dioxan. Scary news: You can find chlorine in most sanitary products. Scarier news: It's tough to spot in the ingredients. However, companies manufacturing products without chlorine (like Seventh Generation and NatraCare) let you know that they're chlorine-free.

Titanium Dioxide: The Jury's Out

Newer to watch lists, titanium dioxide is a white or opaque naturally occurring mineral. Once it is processed, a white, odorless, absorbent substance remains. You'll find it in a wide variety of products, but in cosmetics it whitens, opacifies, or blocks UV rays.

Recent studies have cited it as a carcinogen and photocatalyst (which may be a bad thing, since it's used so often in sunscreen). In addition to sunblocks, you can also find titanium dioxide in toothpastes. Keep your eye on the ingredient list—and on the news, to see what else we learn about this substance.

Spotlight: NaturallyCurly.Com

Did you know half of all women are curly girls? If you're a "curly head," you've spent a good deal of time sussing out the best products to shape your curls the way you like them. Online hair care leader NaturallyCurly.com is here to help. The site organizes an online community to jump-start information and product sharing. It then helps redirect folks to their local stylists, stores, and fellow curlies for ongoing camaraderie and products.

Founded by curl-friends Michelle Breyer and Gretchen Heber, NaturallyCurly.com informs and empowers women, providing styling advice, a shared community, and quality products for curly girls. As their community has become eco-conscious, they've added a green screen to products they carry. NaturallyCurly's recommendations and thoughts for local living help the heads of curlies and straighties alike. Read the following advice from CEO Crista Bailey and cofounder Michelle Breyer on how to stay sustainable and glamorous with your tresses.

What are your favorite product picks for local and sustainable hair care products?

We see more and more manufacturers interested in appealing to earth-loving consumers, so we hope and expect to have broad selection of products to support sustainable living. We also round up local recommendations and aggregate them by community to support curlies throughout their hometowns. Some of our favorite products right now include:

MOP: The MOP brand offers lots of organic ingredients in their product line. And MOP products smell great too. You can find a full line for curls and the straight look.

John Masters: The John Masters line is a complete set of gentle and healthy products filled with organic and natural ingredients. We especially love the non-sulfate shampoo and fortifying conditioners.

Little Sprout: Many of us at Naturally Curly are—very, very—busy moms. We love Little Sprout for babies and up. We all want only the good stuff for our little ones, which means products that are safe and help parents with the dreaded bed head and detangling. Little Sprout can save the day!

Oyin Handmade: This is another great line of natural products that focuses on styling, nourishment, and the health of your hair as well as your skin.

NaturallyCurly.com's core is local community. You can use a myriad of site tools to help you find the best stylists, supply shops, and events in your local community. Check out CurlProducts for product reviews as well as ingredients listings on all products we carry on our CurlMart (*www.curlmart.com*). We also review many items sold in other stores, salons, and drugstores.

What hair care tips can you offer women trying to amp up their sustainable lifestyle?

The first thing to do is to become a label reader. Look for ingredients that you recognize as natural: things like essential oil, plants, herbs, coconut milk, honey, olive oil, and butters. You can guess that if an ingredient is hard to pronounce it is more than likely hard on your hair, too. Remember, hair is super absorbent like our skin, so try to avoid petroleum and petroleum derivatives, phthalates, formaldehyde, parabens, hair dyes with carcinogenic coal tar, and synthetic fragrances.

Look for seals and labels. The key ones for us are:

- ECO-Cert
- USDA Organic
- CSC Compact

Get close to your neighbors by swapping products. Start by trading products that don't work for you instead of throwing them away. Go to NaturallyCurly.com CurlTalk swap board and trade away instead of throwing away products that don't fit for you.

Go to the kitchen. Try your hand at making your own natural hair products. You can find lots of recipes with expertise advice on NaturallyCurly.com CurlTalk.

Buy big. When you can, try to buy liter sizes and use a pump to get every last drop of that product in use. Then, get a refill container to keep reusing your original pump container as much as possible.

It's tough, but use cold water to rinse your hair as much as possible. You save energy and you keep your hair shafts closed and moisturized. Better hair and a better world. That's good stuff.

> "Always remember that true beauty comes from within—
> from within bottles, jars, compacts, and tubes."
>
> —Peter's Almanac

LOOKING GOOD WHILE
LIVING LOCAL

> "The finest clothing made is a person's skin, but, of course, society demands something more than this."
>
> —Mark Twain

Oh, how to handle our second skins? In America, we throw away 68 pounds of clothes and textiles per person per year. Of that textile trash, more than 20 percent of it is considered toxic. How can you best dress to suit yourself and sustain Mama Earth? Start by setting priorities: maximum clothing use, recycled threads, local sources, organic fabrics, and less toxic, low-water-use cleaning strategies.

EYE OPENERS
- Half of the pesticides in nonorganic cotton are considered likely or known carcinogens that can make you and your family sick.
- Children exposed to "cotton poison," methyl parathion, suffer memory loss and emotional swings.
- Eighty percent of energy used to wash clothes in your home goes to heating the water.
- Hot water creates five times more greenhouse gases than cold water does—cool off your water heater and the ozone layer over your slice of the sky.

The Sustainability Screen: Your Closet

Change the World

1. Start Here!

Buy organic cotton, silk, hemp, and bamboo, or recycled fibers and materials

Bring your own shopping bags

Use environmentally safe dry cleaners, or skip it altogether

Wash in cold water with full loads and clothes turned inside-out

Clean your dryer's lint screen after each use and set to proper moisture settings

Use phosphate-free detergents such as Method

3. Reach For It!

Screen brands for fair trade and sustainable materials/processes

Buy from local manufacturers

Use a front-loading washer and dryer

Shift to Energy Star appliances

Skip dyed fabrics—go for natural tones

Skip real and faux (high petro) fur

IMPACT

2. Why Not?

Recycle cleaner's plastic bags and hangers

Send old clothes to secondhand shops or donate them

Try closet swaps with friends

Shop vintage for clothes and accessories

Wash clothes less often (really!)

4. Save for Last!

Make your own clothes

Recycle your clothes into other household goods

Hand-wash clothes with collected rain water

Line-dry clothes

Baby Steps Count

Simple   **EASE TO DO**   Disruptive

THE LOCAL LIFE GUIDELINES

1. *Shopping mantra:* Buy none, buy less, buy used, buy local.
2. *Shop right:* Wear neighborhood threads, minimize your shopping trips, and strip the packaging.
3. *Buy organic fibers and fair trade products:* Good for you and your Mama Earth.
4. *Lean clean:* Choose low-impact washing and drying; learn about sustainable dry-cleaning options.

The Nitty Gritty: Your Shopping

Let's face it: not many of us want to trade off looking good to live locally. Fortunately, you can dress well and "do good."

Buy None, Buy Less, Buy Used, Buy Local

"Buy none" is really a noble goal, but tough to achieve. Perhaps more achievable is buying less and buying used. Your closet offers some of the biggest opportunities to implement the "reuse" and "recycle" Rs so close to our lovely local hearts. We all know about donations to Goodwill and Salvation Army. Put your family on a biannual closet purge to stock some of your family's favorite local causes. A clean sweep equals a clean conscience.

To find appealing used clothing options, explore your neighborhood vintage shops. New to the vintage shop scene? Check out the Shop Locator at FashionDig.com for some of the hippest vintage store options in your backyard. Or try *www.swaporamarama.org* for local swap meets and a series of "how to" classes on remaking your recycled threads. (See the Swap-O-Rama Mamas sidebar for more about swaps.) Still can't find the perfect ensemble in the local vintage haunts? Try *www.Burningtorchinc.com.* They make new clothes out of vintage pieces—stunning, sustainable, and chic.

Keep in mind that jewelry and accessories can be some of the greatest finds via vintage venues. And, if you need a reason to splurge on that sparkling jewel, remember: buying recycled gold saves you three to four times the price point, and buying recycled diamonds saves untold energy and lives—that's the real bling.

→ **Mom to Mom:** ←
Finding a Home for Your Used Clothes

If you can't find a Goodwill (*www.locator.goodwill.org*) or Salvation Army (*www.salvationarmyusa.org*) nearby, or you'd just like to spread around the love, check out CharityGuide.org and CharityNavigator.org Both do a great job of reviewing organizations and how-to's for donations. Learn about charities by cause and community so you can build a long-term relationship with a cause you adore in your hometown. Perhaps you can pick family-oriented charities such as home shelters and housing projects to handle your home's full load. If an international location falls into your definition of local (perhaps a sister city?) you can go global and choose nonprofits that send clothing donations around the world. *Note:* Working Wardrobes (*www.workingwardrobes.org*) outfits U.S. women—many of them single moms—with clothes for job interviews and more. You can find a Working Wardrobes location near you and support your community's women in need.

You may even find you are drawn to more than just the vintage gem. My friend, Renee F., used to shop vintage jewelry and became so enchanted she turned her weekly hunts into bigger and better things. She now buys local, vintage pieces and redesigns them into new adornments. Renee sells her custom pieces around our town throughout local boutiques, city events, and nearby resorts. Visit *www.elizabethdanejewelry.com* for inspiration.

> **Mom to Mom:**
> **Swap-O-Rama Mamas**

If you're game to air a different kind of laundry with your neighbors, or you're just keen on knowing your apparel's former inhabitants, you can keep "vintage" shopping close to home by organizing your own family-to-family clothing swaps and hand-me-arounds.

Pull together a Naked Lady Party to have some fun trading closets. See *www.getcrafty.com/home_nakedlady.php* for inspiration. A night filled with community cocktails, CSA-sourced taste treats, and closet swaps vetted by your hippest friends could take a Mom right back to her pre-children days with a splash more local color. Nice.

Get more bang for your bundle by bringing kids' clothes to the swap too. Kids' clothing swaps are a time-honored Mama tradition that surely must be the genesis of the term "hand me down." Now that many of my Mom friends and I have second ones plus, we turn a regular weekly playdate into a clothes—and toy—swap to keep everyone well outfitted, engaged, and eco-friendly. Don't tell my children, but most of their favorite attire has been especially "well-loved" by playmates—and their siblings—before them.

Once you've reached your maximum thread exchange potential, get local by targeting a backyard-based organization to receive what remains. The company where my husband works, Oakley, partnered up with a neighboring town, Huntington Beach, California, to support one of our local Marine bases, the Camp Pendleton Third Battalion. As part of the program, they throw an annual gala and provide attire for the attending servicewomen and spouses. Working with our women's community service organization (SCJWC), local schools, and parents' groups, my neighbor, Renee, and I collected more than fifty gowns to donate to the gala attendees. Most of those gowns may have eventually made it to a donation site, but plugging into a local cause enabled us to motivate our community to sort through closets full of dresses for people we could imagine walking down our streets. Once you've purged all that can be honestly reused, stash your toss-aways to use as rags. One quick ripping session rivals a massage's stress relief, and you'll feel sustained as you trade in disposable paper towels for reused duds.

Shop Right

Once you've depleted the myriad of reuse and recycle clothing avenues and are moving on to finding new duds, sifting through options with your local screen can be fun. Of course, local stores, farmers' markets, and street fairs offer a number of locally sourced adornments. But expand your search a bit and explore yoga studios, coffee shops, and adventure gear outlets. Consider getting to know local tailors and seamstresses who may do custom work for your family, allowing you to create signature collections and save at the same time.

Or, be brave and join a local knitting circle to craft accessories with personal panache. Research apparel companies located in your 100-mile radius (or whatever your definition of local may be) and seek their gear. We are lucky to have Oakley and a number of other manufacturers grace our closets' backyards. If you look around you may be surprised to find who your corporate neighbors are. Try *www.apparelsearch.com* and *www.fashiondex.com* to search by clothing categories or companies (no geography search as of yet). Or try *www.local.com to* see what companies reside in your Zip Code.

Make a concerted effort to consolidate your shopping. When you're ready to head out and about on a clothing mission, plan in advance to save time and energy—bundle your shopping trips or bundle your online buys. Considering the energy cost of gas versus shipping and packaging, it's probably a sustainability tie whether you shop in stores or online. Just spend a little time aggregating what you need to get the most out of any energy spent.

Be aware of packaging when shopping. All things being equal, pick the naked goods. We throw away literally *tons* of packaging waste a year. Let the folks who make it know that you'd prefer your purchase to be as close to nude as possible. If no nudies, then choose cloth first, paper next, and non-PVC plastics (#1 or #2—check the label) dead last. Many big-box retailers such as Costco, Walmart, and Target are working with vendors to reduce packaging. Reward their efforts and buy the lean and mean goods.

Another broken-record message here, but surprisingly occurring way too infrequently relative to the saturation of the message . . . bring your own bags, bring your own bags, bring your own bags!

Whether you're recycling your past pleasures or aligning your style with a dedicated shopping bag, bringing your own bag leads to sustainability for all things beautiful—trees, water, energy, and fossil fuels. If enough of us bring our bags, perhaps we'll see retailers passing the $1.50 they save from making each one our way. Every little bit counts! To find your signature shopping bag(s), check out *www.emagineGreen.com* for some of the hippest and most practical bag options around. Also spend some time on *www.ReusableBags .com*, the online bag expert. Shop the Modern Totes tab for unique designs. Both the Ecoist (*www.ecoist.com*) and Pristine Planet (*www .pristineplanet.com*) carry a broad line of eco-goods, including plenty of bags. Last—a new thought for many of us—ask your favorite local retailers to recycle bags and hangers. Only 15 percent get recycled— the rest end up in your town's landfills.

Buy Local, Organic Fibers, and Fair Trade Products

When reused and neighborly options leave your closet a wee bit bare, you can still go local with selections. Dressing you and your loved ones is big business. Imagine the market impact you will have as you start demanding that companies' materials, manufacturing, distribution, marketing, and packaging practices meet a sustainability screen. The more you ask for it, the better the products and pricing will get.

Finding Local, Organic Certified, or Fair Trade Certified Products

Understanding how a designer gets ideas from sketchpad to your closet involves knowing the long-term impact of sourcing, manufacturing, and distribution processes. That may involve more time than you've got to give, so here a few guidelines. Scan for pesticide-free, low-energy, low-water-usage farming practices, as well as fair labor practices. Pay attention to manufacturing processes. Many large-scale manufacturers are working to incorporate sustainability-friendly practices into daily production; examples include Gaiam, Nike, Patagonia, PrAna, and Timberland.

What should you be screening for? Water and energy efficiency or carbon-credit offsets; no or low toxic chemical usage; and again, fair labor practices. Target and Walmart carry broad selections of organic cotton and fair trade manufacturers such as the Rogan Jeans for Target, Hanes Organic, Faded Glory (men), No Boundaries (men), Gerber Organic Baby, and Seed Supply Company lines.

Assuming the goods have been made with sustainability practices in mind, think a bit about distribution and marketing practices. Local life guidelines tell us the closer you are to your clothing source, the better. Less travel means less fuel. Companies can use carbon offsets for transportation emissions to help in that area. Choose companies using recycled materials for packaging, such as Timberland. Last, remember also to look for certification from the USDA, Certified Organic Trade Association (CCOF) or Organic Exchange for organic goods, and Fair Trade for fair labor practices.

Buy Organic, Dye-Free Fabrics

It sounds so simple: Sustainability means searching for materials made with as few toxins as possible. Though I understood how synthetic fibers might contain toxins, I was surprised by how many natural-sounding fibers such as cotton and silk often also carry toxins. Farming practices (pesticides) and distribution processes (flying the product around the world to drive it around the United States) as well as packaging supplies contribute to many natural-sounding, but nonorganic, materials bringing toxins to your town, home, and skin. Even with organic fibers, the dyeing process may add toxins. So, give natural colors (white, tan, bone) a try and opt for organic fibers—cotton, silk, hemp, bamboo—when you spice up with colors. For shoes, look for post-consumer tire rubber, insoles from foam cushions, and canvas from old jackets or jeans.

A NOTE ON NO-NO'S

Stay away from fur—not only for animal kindness, but also for the fossil fuels, energy, and water it takes to put one of those backs onto yours. Production of both real and faux furs requires petrochemicals and toxic treatments. If you absolutely cannot part from the furry look, try Loyale Clothing's organic cotton faux fur. Bear in mind that wearing any version of the fuzzy stuff perpetuates a decidedly un-eco fashion statement.

Lean and Mean Cleaning and Storing

Once you've got your goods, you can make them last a long time while ensuring that your community resources do too.

Extending the Life

Get the longest life out of clothes through a couple of quick tips. Treat any stain immediately—use cold water, since hot sets stains. Regularly inspect and sew seams or loose buttons. And, beware overwashing and overdrying. Even cold temperatures will wear out clothes over time. Try wearing body liners. Autrepeau makes a soft, comfy, and seamless liner to keep your clothes free from your "mist" while offering a little help in holding it all together. Check out *www.autrepeau.com*.

Sustainable Cleaning

It's radical, but get everyone in the family to act like a fifteen-year-old guy. Before tossing something into the wash bin, sniff it to make sure it's really too dirty to wear. I'm not advocating going out smelly or spotted, but—perhaps you're not guilty of my former (I promise) sin—give up using the laundry hamper or dry cleaning stack as a clothing repository. When it's truly time to do the wash, follow the guidelines below.

Select Front-Loading Washers and Dryers

Front loaders use about 40 percent less water and less energy. When it's time to buy a new washer, look for Energy Star appliances. We got ours at Best Buy and still salute it each washday.

All washing machines come with a government-provided EnergyGuide rating based on the estimated energy (kilowatts per hour) required to run eight loads of laundry a week. Comparisons rate front loaders versus front loaders (not front loaders versus top loaders). Look for low water use, high efficiency, and high spin speed. Since washers come in sizes from small to big, match your size based on your home's weekly wash requirements. Running a half-full machine wastes energy and water. Last, call your power company and check for available rebates before you buy.

Wash Full, Cold, and Shorter

Since 90 percent of energy used in washing clothes goes to heating the water, washing in cold or warm saves without stinting on clean. You already know that hot water saps colors. Cold water cleans just as well—it requires no extra detergent and keeps clothes looking good longer. Using extra detergent just makes extra bubbles, which take more energy to work though the washer. Try turning clothes inside-out and shortening the wash cycle for even more efficient cleaning. Use your washer's soak setting, or presoak super dirties yourself. If you have a particularly sweaty or stubborn item, coat a quick salt-and-water paste over it to help it shed your "glow."

Wash with Phosphate-Free Detergents

We are lucky to see many sustainably focused brands coming to market. If you live somewhere where your retailers are late to the game, check for detergents sans phosphates. Though they are naturally occurring, phosphates race through the waterways, adding chemicals to the ecosystem and destroying environments for our marine life. Look for Method, Seventh Generation, Ecos, and other earth-friendly brands at your local grocery store, Target, Walmart, or online.

Line Dry or Dry with a Clean Lint Screen Every Time

Though line drying can take up extra space (and seem a bit of a mess), fresh-smelling clothes, long-lasting threads, and a clean conscience reward the efforts. If you can't line dry, you can still save energy and dry your clothes faster than you would otherwise by just pulling out the dryer's little lint screen and tossing away the fuzz before starting up the machine.

Getting the Most from Your Dryer

Heating up the dryer takes most of the energy, so do as many loads back to back as you can and keep the door shut when the dryer's running. Each time you open the dryer, it shuts off and takes five to ten minutes to return to full heat.

Also, use heat sensors or the cool-down (or perm-press) cycle. Only use as much heat as you really need. Heat sensor dryers shut down when clothes are dry. If your dryer doesn't have this feature, shift to cool-down cycle midway through the load. You'll take advantage of residual heat to finish your clothes.

If you don't have a heat sensor dryer now, go with Energy Star when you're ready to buy a new one.

If You Must Dry Clean, Dry Clean Clean

Viewed through a local lens, dry cleaners can provide an easy way to get to know your neighbors. Most are standalone businesses and are places where you're sure to see plenty of folks who live nearby. However, looking through the sustainability screen, the view's a bit darker. At least 85 percent of the 35,000+ U.S. dry cleaners use perchloroethylene (or perc, for short) as a solvent in the dry-cleaning process. Perc is a synthetic, volatile organic compound (VOC) toxic to humans and our world. The EPA has linked perc to organ damage, cancer, and reproductive damage. Since perc enters your system through the air, keeping dry cleaning bagged in your closet increases your exposure.

Though many "dry clean only" garments can be laundered, to be better safe than sorry, opt for a cleaner cleaner. From most sustainable cleaner to least, look for the following.

1. Wet cleaning—professional water-based cleaning of dry-clean garments. This is high-quality cleaning with green stripes: energy efficient, non-polluting, using nontoxic detergents. See *www.earth911.com*

2. CO_2 cleaning—a cleaning process that recycles carbon dioxide (CO_2), compressing it into a liquid that is then used for cleaning. Visit *www.findco2.com* for information.

3. Silicone-based cleaning—also known as "Green Earth" dry cleaning, this process uses a non-perc, silicone-based solvent that isn't as bad as perc, but still causes cancer in rats. See *www .greenearthcleaning.com/rostersearch.asp*.

When you check out cleaners near you, look for those advertising carbon dioxide cleaning or wet cleaning as your first choice. *Remember: Also ask for no plastic bags, and return your hangers to recycle.*

Spotlight: The Gretchen Bleiler Signature Series from Oakley

Carving up the mountain in gear designed with Gretchen Bleiler—can thinking "sustainable" get any cooler? When the Olympic medalist and icon of cool thought about crafting her own snow line with Oakley, she kept an eye on caring for the environment she's enjoyed since childhood. Oakley already supports earth-loving efforts including facility recycling, packaging made from recycled materials, and sourcing power from a renewable energy company (Calpine). But, to support Gretchen's Signature Series, Oakley developed new materials and technology. Women's Brand Director Jennifer Bradley describes the process:

How did Oakley design and build an eco-friendly line with Gretchen Bleiler?

In addition to showcasing her style and sport, Gretchen worked with Oakley to build sustainability into her line's design. Gretchen grew up in Aspen and has been living through shortening ski seasons. Her work on the Signature Series line and with environmental organizations such as *www.StopGlobalWarming.org* are some of the ways she's trying to raise awareness around living a sustainable and local lifestyle.

We created a line of apparel materials made from recycled items called the ECO STORM materials. These textiles come on line through our ECO CIRCLE technology. Manufacturing with ECO CIRCLE processes reduces energy and carbon dioxide emissions by up to 20 percent relative to manufacturing raw polyester. And, we don't use solvents in producing the protective layer, which means fewer toxins get released as women wear the gear and eventually recycle it. In addition to launching the collection in 2008, we began recycling apparel *for our customers*. As women are ready for the next line of Gretchen's Signature Series, they can send us their jackets and pants and we'll recycle them.

Are other sustainability-oriented lines coming soon?

Environmental sustainability has become more and more important to our customers. We're looking at ways to incorporate eco-friendly elements across other lines. The reality is it can still be relatively expensive to offer eco-friendly products. But, because it's a priority for us, our customers, and our athletes, we're committed to finding ways to expand our offering.

We are also working on Gretchen's next collection in order to add an environmental charitable donation into the program. Stay tuned!

What else does Oakley do to support the environment?

In addition to some of the local basics like recycling and rewarding carpooling, we're working to incorporate sustainability principles in our manufacturing and production processes. We recycle manufacturing scrap and hazardous waste. We recycle and shred end-of-line products. And, we use emission control equipment to reduce air pollution. It's an ongoing effort as we learn more about how we can soften our eco-footprint.

> "There is much to support the view that it is clothes that wear us, and not we, them; we may make them take the mould of arm or breast, but they mould our hearts, our brains, our tongues to their liking."
>
> —Virginia Woolf

6

YOUR SUSTAINABLE HOME

> "Home is a place not only of strong affections, but of entire unreserve; it is life's undress rehearsal, its backroom, its dressing room."
> —Harriet Beecher Stowe

In the absence of installing solar panels, what's a local-loving Mama to do to improve sustainability around her home? Quite a lot. Changing your home routine could be the biggest impact your family can have in the quest to enrich your lives and benefit your community. It requires some advance prep, but once you put your home plan in place, big changes result from small efforts.

EYE OPENERS
- The average person spends 90 percent of his or her time indoors.
- The average U.S. home has more than sixty synthetic chemicals throughout the home in cleaners, fabrics, décor, paints, insulation, and so on. These chemicals make up roughly ten gallons of harmful substances in our homes.
- We use 183 gallons of water per person per day (makes drinking sixty ounces seem rather trivial, doesn't it?).
- If each home replaced just one light bulb with an Energy Star bulb, we'd have enough extra energy to light 2.5 million homes.

Standing at your home's threshold and surveying for environmental improvements may overwhelm even the most avid enthusiast. Inhale and start to see your home efforts organized around three major levers: saving water, saving power, and using local and sustainable products. And a bonus: reinforce recycling (see Chapter 2 for details on recycling like a pro).

Start with a Family Board Meeting

Our family uses annual and monthly board meetings—augmented by weekly Sunday night check-ins—to manage our overall family goals and dreams. If you've incorporated a Go Local goal into your version of a family plan, set a baseline (explained later in this chapter) and use your family chore lists and regular "meetings" to track progress. Line up your weekly, monthly, and annual family to-do's to support eco-efforts. Go Local ideas for the family chore list include:

- Living Locally *and* Sustainably Every Day
  - Recycle across the home—home trash, school homework, and car trash.
  - Turn lights off when not in use—indoor and outdoors.
  - Power down all media, electronics, and appliances, and use at-the-source power switches.
  - Use less water—shorten showers and toothbrushing; install low-flow faucets.
  - Pack a "local lunch" using recyclables (and return home with them!).
  - Prep the car to ride green—pack reusable mugs and daily gear bins (see Chapter 7 for details).
- Weekly Sustainability Sweeps
  - Swap a car errand for walking or wheels.

The Sustainability Screen: Your Home

Change
the World

1. Start Here!

Install low-flow adapters on sinks and showerheads

Use cold water in kitchen, laundry, and bath

Turn off the lights

Switch out bulbs to CFL or LEDs

Keep your thermostat at 68 in winter and 75 in summer

Buy recycled paper products and green cleaning products

3. Reach For It!

Install low-flow toilets or put a brick in the toilet tank

Cut showers in half

Check faucets and toilets for leaks

Try timed outdoor watering systems

Install motion sensors and dimmer switches on your lights to reduce power

Switch to alternate energy sources

Buy renewable energy credits (RECs)

Try Energy Star and WaterSense appliances and a tankless water heater

IMPACT

2. Why Not?

Shorten laundry and dishwasher cycles

Skip pre-dishwasher rinse

Sweep instead of spray-washing driveways, patios, and porches

Seal doors and windows to save energy

Switch to soy candles

Choose low VOC paints and finishes

Try organic linens and décor

Look for eco-labels

4. Save for Last!

Solar panel your house: www.readysolar.com

Install your own windmill: www.skystreamenergy.com

Collect rainfall for drip irrigation systems

Run "gray" (used) water outside for irrigation

Baby Steps
Count

Simple   **EASE TO DO**   Disruptive

- Organize carpools for school, activities, and organization meetings — even date night!
- Reinforce use of recycled goods — use recycled items or those made with recycled materials.
- Choose local and sustainable gear, and products with less packaging.
- Give time or resources to a local cause supporting the sustainability of the earth — or at least your town's piece of it.
- Monthly Sustainability Milestones
  - Review utility bills for reduced usage.
  - Review local community investments.
  - Evaluate allowances: "local bonuses," sustainability savings, charitable gifts, and disposable spending.
- Build an Annual Go Local Game Plan
  - Set the family Happy-Go-Local Plan (see Chapter 1 outline).
  - Pick annual sustainability targets: utility savings, local investments, allowance goals.
  - Define daily, weekly, and monthly "dashboards" to track and measure your family's progress.

As you define your family values and priorities, use regular check-in points as a way to stay on track and correct your course when reality varies from original hopes and dreams.

Set a Baseline

Changes around the home take some preparation and dedication. Although one or two big swings (like better recycling or resetting your thermostat) can make a significant impact, a scorecard helps motivate your family to make the long list of little changes. Start with a professional energy and water audit or do one yourself. To do one yourself, try a device like TED—The Energy Detective—to baseline your home energy use; see *www.theenergydetective.com.* Or, skip the gadget and work through a simple checklist. The Daily Green (*www .thedailygreen.com*) and EERE (Energy Efficiency and Renewable Energy group, *www.eere.energy.gov*) both provide detailed checklists you can download to guide you through an audit. To use a professional service, find options near you via these sources:

Home Energy Saver offers auditors by Zip Code: *www.hes.lbl.gov*
EnergyStar.com provides a listing of home auditors by state

Even easier, pull out utility bills and review historical monthly usage. Set a goal to reduce usage 10–15 percent each month, and start tracking family progress.

The Nitty Gritty: Your Home

As you gear up to give your home a sustainability sweep, remember that it's okay to move ahead by moving slowly. Break down your goals into the three major categories—water usage, power usage, and earth-friendly products. Avoid feeling overwhelmed at the enormity of so many local and sustainable home opportunities by setting up small daily steps to pursue.

Save Water . . . Everywhere

Since saving water saves our communities on so many fronts (clean water supply, reduced seasonal temperatures, and improved plant and animal habitats), start room by room to identify how to reduce water use. Your first step to cutting water usage is to install faucet and showerhead flow adapters and aerators. You can reduce your water usage 50–60 percent with nearly invisible impacts on your day-to-day living. Look for products such as Delta Fluidics aerators at *www.energyfederation.org* or at your local home and hardware stores. Can't install these devices? Go low blast on all of your water usage. *If just 2 percent of U.S. homes went low blast instead of full blast when they turned on the faucet, we'd save 12 million gallons of water—per day.*

Next, fix all drips. These can be sneaky. If you get an energy audit, make sure the technician tests your faucets for the slow, silent drips. Want to check yourself? Find your water meter, record the level, and then use no water for an hour. Your meter should read the same at the end of the hour. If it doesn't, you've got leaks. Don't forget to check your toilet for leaks. Lift the tank top and add a few drops of food coloring. If you see the color in the bowl, the toilet is leaking. You can fix the leak yourself (visit DoItYourself.com or Ehow.com for how-to's) or call a plumber to stop your drips.

Finally, if you have the money and the time, install Energy Star appliances and WaterSense faucets and appliances. This goes for the kitchen, too. Although the price tag on these items may give you a start, they will pay for themselves—and then some—with the energy they save over time.

Still need inspiration? Here are a few more water-saving tips, room by room.

The Bathroom

Welcome to the water capital of your world: the bathroom. Do a 360-degree turn in that tiny space to see the biggest water hogs in the house. Multiply that 360-degree turn by the number of bathrooms you have and bask in all the green savings you're about to realize.

Start simple: Turn off the faucet when brushing your teeth and washing your face. You'll save three to five gallons of water each time you remember to do so. To save water and power, consider an at-the-sink tankless heater to heat up your water real-time so you don't run it to do so. Find one on *www.gothotwater.com* or try what we use at home, the Ariston electric water heater, found at *www .tanklesswaterheatersdirect.com* or Home Depot.

If you don't want to spend for an at-the-source water heater or you don't have an obvious space for one near the shower, try a device like the Shower Start Lady Bug. For about $30, this gadget helps you stop wasting water from morning hiccups such as running the shower at full blast to heat and then letting it go a bit too long as you were sucked into a child's outfit debate. The Lady Bug shuts water flow down to a trickle once the water heats up. Not completely guilt-free, but at least it saves a bit of water if you get tangled in morning negotiations.

Prevent drain clogging by installing shower and bath drain strainers. To safely unclog an already sluggish drain, mix equal parts baking soda and water (one-half to one cup each). Pour the mixture down the drain, and let it sit for twenty to twenty-five minutes. Then pour in one and a half quarts of boiling water to open the blockage. Piping fewer drain-cleaner toxins into our waterways means fewer toxins in our soil, fish, air, and—eventually—our bodies.

Install low-flow toilets or place a brick or a gallon-size plastic milk jug filled with water in the toilet tank to reduce water usage. Want to go more high-tech in the *twa-lay*? Four groovy options:

1. *AQUS:* a high-tech design that takes used sink water, stores it, and pumps it to the toilet as needed.
2. *Caroma dual flush toilets:* that's right, designed to flush #1 one way and #2 another.
3. *Clivus Multrum:* for the brave, composting toilets now suitable for in-home use.
4. *Totowashlet:* from our friends in Japan; water spritz and bum heat leave you clean and shiny sans paper.

The Kitchen

One easy step you can start tonight? Use only as much water as you need to cook. Actually measure the water needed for a recipe or tea and coffee and then only use that amount. End the days of eyeballing water level in the pan.

In Chapter 3, you learned about more energy-efficient ways to use your dishwasher. Implementing these practices can save energy—and cut your electricity and water bills.

Finally, when running the sink disposal, use cold water in it. No need to send your pennies (in the form of hot water) down the drain unnecessarily.

Outdoors

It happens outside, so you may not see it. However, typical outdoor home and garden water use can waste buckets and buckets of our precious stuff. Use timed watering systems for lawn and garden care. Water only as long as needed and at cooler times of day (early morning or late evening) so water doesn't evaporate as you're watering. Didn't your Mom always tell you a little elbow grease was a good thing? Here's a chance to share the bounty with your children: Sweep instead of spraying-washing driveways and patios. Water no more than once every five to six days. And, skip watering altogether when it's windy, since the wind blows water off your thirsty yard and into streets and drainpipes.

Save Power

Focus on power savings to shrink your family's carbon footprint. Shifting to alternate energy sources, more efficient lights, lukewarm living, and greener appliances cuts CO_2 emissions and shaves dollars off your utility bills.

Go for Alternate Energy Sources

Find your state's local power and sustainability options. Good news: More than thirty states have an alternate energy source option. Go to your utility company website, enter your Zip Code, and check for renewable sources. For most options and homes, the incremental monthly price can be relatively small: $10–$20 per month. Check out The Power Network at *www.eere.energy.gov/greenpower* for more information.

If you're out of luck in your city or state, you can still support the cause. Buy renewable energy credits (RECs) to enable a small-scale, alternate energy provider to compete with conventional, large-scale power companies. An REC acts as a price subsidy. Buying $20 worth of wind energy RECs allows a wind company to reduce its price by $20 in order to match large-scale power sources. By doing this, you help alternate power source companies grow and build large-scale offerings to eventually match competitor pricing on their own. Plus, you get a lot more green energy going out there. Try *www.green-e.org* for RECs in each state.

Want to mastermind your power usage? Check out *www.Grid Point.com.* Geared more toward high-tech energy optimizers than efficiency-oriented penny savers, GridPoint acts as your home energy analytic wizard and automated procurement officer. The system integrates with power sources and your home. It notes your energy patterns, accesses alternate power sources, stores energy from off-peak usage times, resells energy to reduce your cost, and logs backup energy sources for down times.

Whew. Sounds like mission control—or HAL. Either way, worth checking out if you've got the resources.

For a lower-cost energy monitor, try the Digital PowerCost Monitor—$185 at *www.powermeterstore.com.*

THE TAXMAN

Did you know you can get up to $2,000 in tax credits as well as "green mortgages" and loans to help your sustainability efforts? Buying renewable energy credits can also earn tax deductions. EnergyStar. gov covers the nuts and bolts of tax credits available from the Emergency Economic Stabilization Act of 2008. This act extended tax credits for improving home energy efficiency as well as solar energy systems. In addition, it added tax credits for wind energy systems and plug-in hybrid electric vehicles. You can earn tax credits for things like installing energy-efficient doors and windows, adding insulation, upgrading a water heater, or investing in solar power options. Go to *www.EnergyStar.gov* or *www.planetgreen.com* for details.

If your home meets a specific set of energy-efficiency criteria (as defined by the Home Energy Rating Source), you may qualify for a "green mortgage." Although the mortgage is not necessarily cheaper, you may qualify for a larger loan because the underwriter calculates the energy savings against the mortgage costs. To qualify, you will need to do an energy audit, which can cost a few hundred dollars (many lenders will roll this into the loan cost as well). Many banks also offer cash credits off a loan's closing costs for energy initiatives such as complying with Energy Star guidelines. Check with your lender.

Lights, Please

Turn off the lights—obvious, so help your family remember to do so. We use a star sticker on highly trafficked switches. You can get fancy with a sticker made by One with the Earth; with an Earth illustration and a "Please turn off the lights" call out, it's cool, effective and—the best part—free! Order at *www.agshen.org/freestickerorder info.html.* Can't seem to turn the lights off? Install motion sensor and timer lights. To further cut back on energy used for lighting, replace conventional bulbs with as many CFLs (compact fluorescent lights) or LEDs (light emitting diodes) as you can.

One CFL 20-watt bulb shines like a 110-watt incandescent light. CFLs are still a bit more expensive than incandescent, but last eight times longer. One caveat: they have traces of mercury, so dispose via your hazardous waste collection process. LED bulbs are coming online in a large way. New to the mass market, they're starting to sell at reasonable prices. They're 90 percent more efficient than conventional incandescent lights and can last up to 100,000 hours. Eleven years of power—that's a deal.

A watch-out for all energy-saver bulbs: If you have sensor or dimmer lights, make sure you buy CFLs and LEDs specifically tagged as "sensor" and "dimmer" safe. Otherwise, CFLs and LEDs can be fire hazards for sockets wired for incandescent lights.

Want to learn more about green lighting? Go to *www.nvisioncfl .com.* A few final tips: Try a solar powered rechargeable flashlight from *www.HybridLight.com* or a solar powered light—the Magic Globe—which brightens the outdoors with multicolor options. Above all, don't forget to use natural light—open the curtains.

Hot and Cold

Keep your home comfy, but efficient. Set your thermostat set at 68 degrees or lower in the winter and 75 degrees or higher in the summer. Try timed thermostats that turn heat off at bedtime and back on an hour before rising. Seal doors and windows to keep hard-earned energy (which equals hard-earned cash) inside. You can find easy-to-use sealants at Home Depot and Lowe's.

A low-cost way to amplify your efforts is to flip your fan. When run in reverse, ceiling fans push warm air down and pull cool air up. Also remember that heat pumps and natural gas furnaces are much more efficient than space heaters. Avoid space heaters as much as you can.

Keep AC and heating systems efficient by buying permanent filters and cleaning them twice a year. Don't know where the filter is or how to change it? Try your owner's manual to learn how to do it yourself, or budget roughly $100 for a service call. If you don't want to switch to permanent filters, remember to replace the disposables twice a year. Amp your savings with better insulation. Try Green-Fiber Cocoon, which is made from recycled materials and easily used for re-insulating homes.

Pay attention to your fireplace. Shut the flue when it's not in use to keep it from sucking heat and cold up and out the chimney. According to the EERE, an open flue accounts for up to 15 percent of your energy loss. When you use the fireplace, get cozy with coffee in your hearth. Look for javalogs (*www.java-log.com*), which are made from recycled coffee grounds to burn cleaner than wood.

Recruit the great outdoors to help save energy. Do you need warmth or cold most often? Pay attention to southern exposures if you want a cooler home and northern exposure if you want warmer. Paint cool areas darker colors to warm them up, and warm areas brighter colors to cool them down. Looking for an excuse to indulge? Install radiant floor heating. Oh, so efficient and oh, oh, oh so nice.

Appliances

Want to know how much power your appliances consume? Try the Kill A Watt Electricity Meter. For $40 you can track power use and cost for any appliance. Try *www.p3international.com to* buy yours. Fine-tune home appliances to lighten your load. Remember the basics: Use appliances during off-peak hours (between 10 P.M. and 7 A.M.) and run them on cool cycles as much as possible.

When it comes to the big energy gulper anchoring the kitchen (also known as the fridge), aim to keep it full and set to 37°F (keep the freezer at 5°F). Can the closed door hold a piece of paper? If not, your fridge is leaking cool air. Clean fridge gaskets and condenser coils twice a year. Don't know what those things are or how to clean them? They're in back or on the bottom behind a panel. I looked in our owner's manual, gave it whirl, and then decided to pay the $80 service fee twice a year.

For smart cooking, remember to choose the microwave first, then the toaster oven, then the big oven. Turn off the oven 10–15 minutes before cooking time ends—it will remain hot and continue cooking. On the stove, cook with pot and pan lids on. Replacing your stove? Go gas; it emits half the emissions as electric (and remember to check Energy Star ratings).

Next, introduce yourself to the water heater. Wrap it up in an insulating jacket (you can buy one at your local hardware store to keep it warmer. Set temp to 120°F max.

Better bet: consider a tankless water heater. We installed the Notanku brand and like it. Takagi also comes with kudos from Josh Dorfman, a.k.a. *The Lazy Environmentalist* radio show host and book author (an excellent resource). Also check out Noritz, Rinnai, and Bosche. For an overview of how tankless water heaters work and what to look for in installation read *www.eere.energy.gov* and *www.tanklesswaterheaterguide.com*.

Sustainable Products:
Cleaners Good for You and Mama Earth

You want nontoxic, phosphate- and chlorine-free, biodegradable, nonpetroleum, fragrance- and dye-free, vegetable-based cleaners. Whew! To make your own, you need only baking soda, distilled white vinegar, lemons, salt, and club soda (use the home soda club maker to make your own; see *www.sodastreamusa.com* for details).

Best do-it-yourself natural home cleaners according to *www.GreenLivingIdeas.com*:

Baking soda: a scouring cleaner and a clothing and carpet deodorizer.

Washing soda: (sodium bicarbonate): deodorizes and cuts oil (such as grease and wax). Can be harsh on the hands, so use gloves.

White vinegar and/or lemon juice: dissolves surface grease and grime buildup

Lavender, tea tree, clove, and grapeseed extracts: disinfect and ward off fungi.

Making your own not working out? You can still shop local stores to find many organic, nontoxic brands that make "clean" cleaning easy for you. Check out Seventh Generation, Method, Green Earth, Ecover, Planet, and Mrs. Meyers, available at most grocery stores and Target nationwide. Or try celeb Ed Begley's line, Begley's Best, at *www.begleysbest.com.*

Mrs. Meyers makes a great starter kit with four small spray bottles in a six-pack-style box—perfect size for little hands to help.

SQUEAKY-CLEAN SLEUTH

Trying to decide what cleaners to clear out and which to keep? Check the Household Product Database at the National Institutes of Health website (*www.householdproducts.nlm.nih.gov/search.htm*) or the Cleaners Solutions database at *www.cleansersolutions.com* to find out what's brewing in your cleaning products. Remember to dispose of unwanted cleaners via hazardous waste drop-off.

Paper Products

If you must use disposable items, cut back use and choose recycled, Forest Stewardship Council (FSC) certified supplies. Go for recycled paper everything—towels, napkins, toilet paper and so on. Again, Seventh Generation and Ecos have broad lines in national distribution. And speaking of paper, if every home swapped one twelve-pack of their usual toilet paper for recycled product, we'd save 5 million trees and 17,000 garbage trucks worth of waste. Try it. The TP's gotten much smoother. Check out *www.shitbegone.com* to learn more about toilet paper than you ever thought you wanted to know—and to buy the good stuff in bulk.

Setting the Table

Need disposable plates and cutlery? Try bamboo. Bamboo veneer brands are in many stores or available online in bulk. Check *www.sinlessbuying.com* for a broad selection of eco-friendly disposables. And try Bagasse—found at *www.branchhome.com*—for recyclable cups and plates.

BAMBOO AND SOY

Bamboo has popped up as an Earth savior. Clothes, flooring, and picnic plates all come in eco-friendly bamboo. Soy also earns sustainability kudos as petroleum-based wax and dairy foods alternative. Folks have raised the question of whether or not all of this green adulation has a reverse effect—overharvesting and global transport seem rather un-eco. The net answer is that bamboo and soy highlight the reality of sustainability efforts: perfection doesn't exist, but better and better solutions and good intentions do. At this point, bamboo and soy still seem to be an Earth-saving plus. But, you may want to check the source of some of your bamboo and soy and shoot for crops closer to home when you can.

When you buy flatware, consider passing on silver and going for stainless steel instead. It's a renewable resource and dishwasher safe.

Linens and More

Once you've shed your clothes, keep wrapping your body in local and organic fibers. Look for towels and bedding made from organic cotton, hemp, silk, and bamboo. Wash your duvet covers once a week, or once a month if you use a top sheet. Wash duvets once a year or once every three years if you use a top sheet. Dry with tennis balls to reduce clumping. Last, try to shift out of plastic (PVC-laden) shower curtains and into hemp or organic fibers.

Furniture and Décor

Put your finishing sustainability touches to work. Haunt community events and street fairs to find décor and furnishings exuding your hometown feel. Look for furniture recycled via consignment stores as well as neighborhood rummage, estate and—oh, all right— garage sales. When buying new pieces, search for items made out of recycled materials, organic fibers, and Forest Stewardship Council (FSC) certified lumber.

Look to soften and warm a room with soy candles. Conventional candles come from paraffin. Paraffin comes from . . . boo, petroleum. Soy burns 90 percent cleaner, 50 percent longer, and shines brighter as a renewable resource. No soy candles in your local stores? Try the next-best step: look for cotton wicks, which burn cleaner that those made with a zinc core. And, remember beeswax candles offer a sweet smelling substitute as well. To light the candles, opt for cardboard matchbooks over lighters and matchboxes.

For interior paints and other surface finishes, choose those that have low or no VOCs (volatile organic compounds). Conventional paints release VOCs—which are toxins—while they're on your wall. Recommended brands include Benjamin Moore's EcoSpec line, Anna Sova (0-voc and 99 percent food-grade ingredients; scent-enhanced options), Olympic premium interior paint (0 voc; 1,000 shades at Lowe's), American Clay's plasters (a Zen touch: emits negative ions, which balance positive ions of daily life such as dust, electronics and pollution), and AFM *www.afmsafecoatpaint.com* (0 voc).

Building an outside walkway or driveway? Use tile or gravel instead of asphalt. The grooves and spaces collect water so it can be absorbed back into the ground instead of washed away down the street.

THE RUMMAGE SALE GOES UPSCALE

Swaps are not just for closets. Remember your church or school rummage sales? With a little advance planning, you can take the rummage sale up a notch by incorporating gently used furniture and décor. Turn the event into an all-day block party to find a new home for your no-longer-needed accents and to make your neighborhood a bit more homey. Put the word out to folks a few weeks in advance, set the date, guesstimate your inventory, and rotate sign-ups for local feasts and treats. Open the event an hour early for neighbor "pre-shop-swaps" and then let the sale begin. Put proceeds toward the next block party. A spring cleaning rummage sale can tee up an excellent July 4 neighborhood bash.

Spotlight: emagineGreen

Very busy Mom and successful entrepreneur Tonya Ensign first absorbed details about the impact of global warming from an Oprah Winfrey show playing in the background of her day. As she heard plain-speak statistics and practical solutions, she began to percolate a high-impact way to address local living and sustainability. Tonya saw an opportunity to raise families' awareness around environmental concerns as well as support women interested in building their own businesses.

With a few other busy moms, Tonya founded emagineGreen. Emerging as the direct sales leader for earth-loving products and environmental education for consumers, emagineGreen helps people convert sustainability concerns into measurable impact. Epitomizing her whole-life commitment to "being the change you want to see," Tonya and her predominantly female team offer women a way to pursue meaningful work that truly makes a difference, on a flex-time model that centers around their community. Primarily through an at-home, direct sales model, emagineGreen coaches bring information, products, and results tracking to your efforts toward increasing your family's shade of green

What is emagineGreen, and how does it support helping the environment?

Our guiding principle at emagineGreen is "Awareness + Action = Impact." We see our mission as turning curiosity about what is happening in our environment into positive action. We simplify the "going local" or "being sustainable" process for millions of people who want a healthier home and environment. Together, we hope to bring about a change in how our culture interacts with our environment and precious natural resources by reducing our ecoFootprint. We want to be, inspire, and help others become sustainability role models for our families and communities. And, we see voting with our consumer dollars as one of the most effective ways to create a more sustainable way of life.

How can interested moms get involved in emagineGreen?

Moms can get involved in any of three ways: Shop our website or catalog for products which facilitate a sustainability screen; host an eco-party where an emagineGreen coach provides local lifestyle how-to's as well as product options; or help lead the change, by becoming an emagineGreen coach. Go to emagineGreen.com to learn more.

"There is nothing like staying at home for real comfort."

—Jane Austen

7

A MOM NEEDS TO DRIVE: YOUR WHEELS

> "The civilized man has built a coach, but has lost the use of his feet."
> —Ralph Waldo Emerson

With every gallon of gas consumed churning out twenty-four pounds of greenhouse gases, it's no wonder transportation generates *a third to a half* of all man-made carbon dioxide emissions. That's no good for anyone's backyard. Today's average annual vehicle miles per year is four times what it was just ten years ago. One of the surprising—albeit obvious—observations about living the local life will be how much less driving you *need* to do when you focus on fueling your life closer to home. However, for most of us, driving is still a reality. In this chapter, you'll find ways to set up your mobile routine to cut miles, maintain vehicles to lower your GPG (guilt per gallon) and increase MPG, and start taking steps toward wheel-less transportation. Trading out a few driving errands for walking adventures and downshifting your wheels even a little bit can leapfrog local and sustainable goals.

EYE OPENERS
- The average U.S. vehicle miles per year, per person, is twice the per-person average in other *developed* nations.

- We guzzle 500,000 gallons of petroleum per person per year.
- One second (pause—that's *one second*) of high-powered driving creates as much greenhouse gas as thirty minutes of normal driving (at the speed limit without a lot of starts and stops).
- Driving at 75 mph versus 65 mph decreases fuel efficiency by 15 percent.

The Sustainability Screen: Your Wheels

Change the World

1. Start Here!

Get local, local

Maintain your car's tires and fluids

Drive smart—more slowly with less stops and starts

Find out if your car can run on alternative fuels

Buy a TerraPass to offset your car's emissions

Swap three car-powered errands a week for foot power

3. Reach For It!

Shift to a hybrid car or higher MPG option

Cluster kids' activities around reduced drive times

Swap one commute a week for public transportation, carpooling, or car sharing

IMPACT

2. Why Not?

Try Better World Club roadside assistance

Stock the car to support recycling; use reusable mugs/cups

Lighten your load while driving— organize for daily car loads

Turn the car off when idling more than thirty seconds

4. Save for Last!

Try a biodiesel or biofuel car

Go sans car

Shift to electric-powered vehicles

Store an alternative fuel source at home

Convert your gas-guzzling engine to electric (takes ten grand and a lot of expertise)

Baby Steps Count

Simple   **EASE TO DO**   Disruptive

THE LOCAL LIFE GUIDELINES FOR YOUR WHEELS

1. *Draw your circle:* Localize your outings.
2. *Embrace your inner power:* Use the family's feet to walk, run, and pedal around.
3. *Put your feet up:* Try public transport.
4. *Share the ride:* Carpooling, clustering to-do's, car sharing, and more.
5. *Same wheels, greener rides:* Car maintenance to soften your blow.
6. *Setting up an eco-friendly home on the road:* Sustainability tips for your rides.
7. *Go for greener wheels:* Electric, hybrids, alternative energy fuels, and gas MPG stars.
8 *TerraPass—your "Get out of eco-jail (almost) free!" card:* Carbon dioxide credits calculated real time from your car habits.

The Nitty Gritty: Your Wheels

With the daily Sherpa duties that kids, carpools, and pets create, most moms can't swear off their wheels or swap SUVs for Priuses anytime soon. And, even in periods of record gas prices, the gas savings from a hybrid versus the cars' premium pricing often takes more than a few years to pay back. What's a local-loving Mama to do? Better car care, some interior reorganization, and creative scheduling can downshift your transportation footprint to be a wee bit more Mini Cooper and a lot less big rig.

Arguably an area of our life where we most tangibly create CO_2, our car lives can be a conundrum. Moms and families need to find a realistic balance between necessary convenience and big changes to reduce CO_2 emissions. Keep in mind that implementing even one or two of the following ideas counts as taking real steps down a sustainable path. Don't let the breadth of opportunities overwhelm your intention to try a few changes.

Draw Your Circle: Localize Your Outings

You probably already set your definition of "local" as you explored earlier chapters. For this exercise, shrink your circle to five miles from your home or workplace. Use Google Maps to visualize what your circle looks like and then search for businesses within your hub. You may be surprised at how many daily errands you run by habit that are a bit too far from reach. When you tighten your focus—perhaps even a little bit more, to three miles—you'll reap rewards of sustainable living and saved time. If you live in an area where the closest grocery store is more than five miles and the library is in another town, bear in mind the goal is simply to tighten up your radius. Going from twelve miles to ten miles in the countryside or small towns can be just as high impact as going to a three-mile radius in suburbia.

Download your errand spots, carpool locations, doctor's offices, and even shopping and lunch places onto a list, and then systematically swap those that are out of your chosen radius with options that are within it where possible. Once you've remapped your daily life, work through the following tips to keep increasing your family's sustainability efforts.

Walk, Run, and Pedal

This may be seemingly impossible for the family chauffeur, but dare yourself and your family to replace a few car errands a week with feet. Exercise, reduced carbon footprints, and maybe a few less purchases will be your reward. Challenge older kids to pick a weekly errand to cover via bikes or old-fashioned walking. Still have one in the stroller? Unload the toys and open up space for a grocery store run. Vary the family routine a bit to follow dinner with a thirty-minute stroll and swing by the dry cleaner's. Slightly shift everyone's presumption to drive and you advance your sustainability path.

As you power up your ped cause, suit up in comfy but practical gear (think pockets). If you don't love local options, check out national companies such as Patagonia, Stella, and Gaiam, which create—with an eye to Mother Earth's longevity—a myriad of good trailblazing attire. Sling a backpack (carrying a few shopping bags and a reusable bottle of filtered water) over your shoulder, strap on eco–friendly kicks (see *www.zappos.com* for a broad selection), and strut out into the wild local yonder.

Want to go really wild? Try a solar powered backpack or armband (Voltaic, Lil'Amp, or 'Lectra for backpacks and Holio for armbands) to recharge your cell phone or iPod while you walk. REI has a great selection as well.

Need to cover more ground? Bicycles await. Consider pulling a child-carrier trailer on your bike to carry cargo for your errands. Try *www.bicycletrailers.com* for excellent reviews of a wide range of trailer options. To quote Bill Strickland, author of *Make the Impossible Possible,* "The bicycle is the most efficient machine ever created: Converting calories into gas, a bicycle gets the equivalent of three thousand miles per gallon."

Tree Hugger and The Lazy Environmentalist both have excellent overviews of the best bikes for urban crawls. And *www.ibike.org* covers gear, bike statistics, trails, and vacation options—globally.

Feeling a little lazy? Try an electric bike. Check out *www.electric-bikes.com.* They can go 500 to 2,500 miles on one charge.

Give Public Transport a Chance

Public transportation viability varies based on your hometown. Every city differs. Buses, subways, trains—much to choose from, with sometimes mixed appeal. Still, it's worth a try. Public transport offers sustainability solutions and adds some oomph to your productivity. Work, read, or relax while someone else gets you there. Even if it takes a tad bit longer to get where you're going, less stress on the way is bound to improve your mindset as you jump into the day. That's reason enough to exchange one stop-and-go, horn-honking, can-you-believe-he-just-cut-me-off-like-that commute a week.

Navigating Public Transport with Wee Ones

Consider using a body carrier instead of a stroller. With the right fit and a little practice, they make bus, subway, or even airport travel much easier to navigate. Friend and Mom of three, Allison B., swears by the body carriers and forgoes a stroller for any outings except workout runs. I used slings, wraps, chest packs, and backpacks with both of my children from the time they were newborns until age three. I've even "double-bagged" them with a sling around front for my youngest and a Ergo baby carrier for my oldest. Admittedly this keeps shopping acquisitions limited, but you save money and gain speed, efficiency, and a bit of workout. If you absolutely need to carry home a large load of loot, consider skipping the dual versions of strollers and stick with just a jogging stroller instead of the standard stroller. Though often a pound or two heavier, these strollers usually collapse and extend more quickly with a one-hand hold to make doorway entry and exit less stressful. The Mountain Buggy brand even makes a side-by-side double stroller narrow enough to fit through a standard door. Visit OCtravelTykes.com for a comprehensive product offering of carriers and strollers as well as helpful product reviews. Friend and Mom of two, Keli Johnson, built the site to make stroller selection easier for women with limited time (a.k.a. mothers).

To learn more about your public transport options, go to *www.publictransportation.org* or try *www.greyhound.com* for buses, *www.subways.net* for subway scoop, and *www.amtrak.com* for railway rides.

If your city doesn't have a public transport option you can tolerate, think about getting involved in the cause to put one in place. Try *www .votesmart.org* and *www.congress.org* to learn about local leaders, their platforms, and ways to get your initiatives on their priority list.

Share the Ride

Moms mastered the kids' carpool eons before people knew to hug trees. A few reminders about one of Mom's best inventions:

Cluster your kids: As the youngest of four, my husband can't remember ever playing on a team in "his" age group. Though it doesn't work for every child or every family, consider clustering your children's activities and teams by their ages and interests to simplify logistics. Stare down the weekly schedule, bundle events by location and likely carpools, and then see where you can either combine kids in one class or reduce the extracurriculars in your fight for a few less trips.

Trade skill sets with the other parents: If you work out of your home and can't help as easily with the driving, trade something else like snack prep, phone calling duties, or fundraiser donations to get your young ones equitably on the weekly carpool routes.

Publish the weekly plan: Once you've negotiated the activities with your family and routes with your friends, publish the driving plan for all to see: on the fridge, via e-mails, and in your calendar. Recruiting your spouse to cover shifts and run errands during commutes counts for sustainability plan points and time savings for you.

Does your commute have you stressed out? Consider the bliss of the HOV (high occupancy vehicle, or carpool) lane . . . faster to and fro and less chaos en route. Though your kids' carpools run without a hitch, your work commute may still be a bit bumpy. If you can't set up a suitable carpool partner via your office or social networks, several websites sit ready to serve you:

- *www.Carpoolworld.com*
- *www.Erideshare.com*
- *www.Rideshare.511.org*

Car Sharing

A bit more radical, but still an option: try car sharing or rent a car by the hour to drive down your driving impact. Here are just a few of many options out there.

Car Sharing: an excellent resource of worldwide car sharing networks. *www.carsharing.net.*
Zip car: sets up hourly and daily rentals in major cities—Boston, New York, San Francisco, DC, and more to come. *www.zipcar.com.*
Flexcar: also sets up short-term rentals in major cities—Atlanta, Los Angeles, Portland, San Francisco, San Diego, Seattle—with plans to expand to thirty cities. *www.flexcar.com.*

Trying to toggle between a work carpool and kids' schools and activities may defy reality. The goal need not be 100 percent replacement—shoot for one time a week. Baby steps make a difference.

Car Maintenance to Soften Your Environmental Blow

No Mom has time for car trouble. A day without wheels creates a week full of hassles. Fortunately, keeping your car in tip-top shape delivers on your sustainability plan too.

Use the following maintenance checklist as a monthly green road map. Also consider a switch to Better World Club (BWC) for roadside assistance. Although AAA leads the market, BWC offers the same great service with an eco-screen as its filter. BWC also donates $1 per transaction to green causes. Check out *www.betterworldclub.com* for more information.

Maintenance is the key to keeping your car running at maximum performance and minimal impact. Above all, keep your tires fully inflated—doing so saves 3 percent or more on your gas mileage and reduces greenhouse gases (GHGs) released. Plus, your tires last longer, which saves you money and earns stars for your living local goals to buy less.

I defer to filling station expertise, but you can check your tires yourself. Look on your driver-side door or in your car manual to find your tires' recommended pounds PSI (per square inch), and check the pressure at the gas station. If it's low, pump. Need your own tire gauge? Try the Accu-gauge—*www.ghmeiser.com*.

Need new tires? Consider retreads. It takes a third less fossil fuels to make them versus new tires and—bonus—they cost less. Check out *www.retread.org/Guide* for a database of brands and locations. The EPA gives good guidelines as well at *www.epa.gov/cpg/products/retread.htm*.

Want to know how much carbon dioxide emission your tires generate? Check out *www.cleancommuteva.org/calculator.html* for a calculator.

Also keep track of your car's fluid levels—and what type you're putting into your car. Ask for refined motor oil next time you change the oil (you *do* change the oil every 3,000 miles, right?). Recycle motor oil at your service center. It's immortal.

When it comes to antifreeze, buy the kind made with propylene glycol antifreeze. Propylene glycol is biodegradable, relatively nontoxic, and long-lasting. Many brands are available at most service centers, but you have to ask.

Always a pain, but still better than letting it go too long—take your car in for its regularly scheduled checkups. Those tweaks and adjustments keep your car running smoothly and your community cleaner. For a booster shot of feel-good local living, budget the time to meet your service station and/or repair shop owner and chief mechanic. It's a lovely blast from the past to be greeted by the gas station team. And, you may feel more comfortable about firing away with all maintenance questions once your know the face spouting back recommendations.

Pull car washing off the family's chore list to make room for a different eco to-do (maybe the hazardous waste drop-off?). Swap the do-it-yourself commercial car washes or at-home driveway washes for a professional job. They use less water and fewer chemicals (and you'll put a smile on your neighbor's face by eliminating the sudsy runoff). Keep this in mind when it comes time for the perennial car wash school fundraiser. Try a recycling fundraiser instead.

Good for your mindset and good for your mundo: Drive slowly and accelerate slowly. Quick-trigger driving reduces fuel efficiency and increases GHGs. At 75 mph you create 15 percent more pollution than at 65 mph. Set yourself up for success—leave ten minutes early. Need help taming your inner Trixie Speed Racer urges? Set your car to cruise control. The ideal maximum is 60 mph.

And, if you're stopped more than fifteen seconds, turn your car off. Idling churns GHGs. Time your regular traffic stops; your wait may surprise you.

Consider what your car is carrying that might be impeding your car's performance. Pass on roof racks—wind resistance reduces efficiency. Trunk bike racks have the same effect, but to a lesser degree.

At the risk of sounding comical, if not downright impossible, try not to use your car as an all-purpose ready-for-anything storage container. The heavier your wheels, the less fuel-efficient your ride. Find tips and how-to's in the next section.

When it comes to fuel, use the lowest-octane gas you can. Only one in ten cars really needs higher-octane gas. Check your owner's manual and make sure your car really requires (versus "recommended that you use") the more expensive stuff.

Setting up a Sustainable Home-on-the-Road

You can transform your car interior from a chaotic trash bin to a pristine eco-accelerator with a little advance preparation and perhaps a lot of kid coaching. Take stock of your car's layout, your regular routes, and your tolerance for daily setup/teardown. Pick what fits from the following options to ease the impact of daily drives.

Dig too deeply and you'll see we've all got napkins, old home-work, to-go cups, and a few "unidentifiables" in our cars. Consider a simple recycling setup to keep the car clean and landfills lean. In the front seat, attach a small bag to the passenger seat for recyclables (try a permanent one like OmniPeace 4 in 1 bags from *www.earthwise bags.com* or biodegradable bags such as BioBags, available at many grocery stores and food co-ops). Also hang bags from the back of the front seats and tag one "recyclables" and one "trash." Fill and unload as needed.

You know to bring your own bags, carry a portable coffee mug, and trade disposable water bottles for reusable ones. However, having them all at the right moment is a different story. Stash mugs and bottles near your passenger seat in a storage container and keep all of your bags inside one of the bigger bags in your trunk. As you unload groceries, stuff all the bags back in the biggest bag again and place them at the front door to make sure they make it back into the car. Remember a great option, the Envirosax, available at *www .emagineGreen.com*. They fold up tiny, but open up big for weekly grocery loads—and you can stuff five in one compact bag that fits in one of your door storage pockets.

MEALS FOR MOMS

A number of my friends and I had babies within months of each other. Women set the bar as excellent advocates and supporters of each other, and few things bring this strength to light like the birth of a new baby. Girlfriends all over come through with big-sibling toys, last-minute new baby Halloween costumes, and the oh-so-needed-and-beloved New Baby Mommy Meal.

Support sustainability as well as the new mamas by delivering the meals packaged in reusable bags and prepped in recyclable aluminum or reusable glass (your name written on the bottom with a permanent marker makes it easy for the sleep-deprived Mom to return containers to the correct home). Tuck in a set of reusable shopping bags to help a weary woman stay on a sustainable course. Remember *www .bhappybags.com* for bag options sure to lift spirits.

Feel like you have to carry half your house in the car in order to save drive time? It's hard to keep all the weekly gear, information, and "contingency" items on hand without having them in the car. How can you reduce your load without reducing your efficiency?

Divide your current carload of items into "Daily Must Haves" and "Need Some Days of the Week." For example, your Daily Must Haves might include your gym bag, reusables, specific kids' gear (such as sunblock or spare diapers), and music. The Need Some Days of the Week list picks up kids' activity gear (such as dance class or soccer equipment) and pet items.

Carve out space in the trunk for the Daily Must Haves. For other items, set up a bin for each day of the week in the garage. Everyone in the family loads the next day's bin the night before with whatever items they'd like in the car. Start each day with that day's bin and switch it out at night. Not only do you reduce your load, you also enlist everyone's help in making morning exits run a bit more smoothly. *Bonus efficiency points: Load the backpacks and lunch bags the night before too.*

Go for More Sustainable Wheels

Although the best way to keep focused on a local lifestyle is by eliminating driving, you can still add to sustainability efforts when it's time to replace a vehicle. Read on for a primer on energy savers on the road.

Remember to ask your local car insurance provider if the company offers discounts for alternate energy vehicles. If they don't, consider changing to one who does, like Farmer's Insurance, which offers a 10 percent discount.

Looking to burnish your hip and cool Mom image? Go for a hybrid motorcycle—eCycle and Kneeslider are both deep in development. Need one NOW? Try the Enertia rechargeable motorcycle. It's 90 percent cleaner than fossil fuel cars, four times as efficient as the leading hybrids, and even twice as efficient as electric cars.

Flex Fuel Vehicles (FFV)

These engines can run on gasoline or on a brew of 85 percent ethanol and 15 percent gas called E85. Your car may be a flex fuel vehicle and you don't even know it. Check the label inside your fuel latch, or check *www.e85fuel.com*. Your car will run well on ethanol, but will be 20 percent or so less fuel-efficient, so plan accordingly. Go to *www.e85fuel.com* to find ethanol stations near you.

Biodiesel — What Would Willie Do?

Also know as "clean" diesel, biodiesel comes from vegetable oil. Legendary life adventurer Willie Nelson runs his fleet of buses and other vehicles from his own multigallon tank in Luck, Texas. We're waiting to hear that Bruce Springsteen does too.

Sadly for rock-star Mamas, no biodiesel mini-van options are available yet.

Keep ears open and eyes peeled for the ever-advancing sci-fi transport options soon becoming our reality. Electric cars like the Tesla and Electric Syper will accompany versions coming from Honda, Toyota, and Chevrolet in the near term. Hydrogen-powered cars are becoming real options as well as a few new technologies such as the Going Green GWiz car (currently available in London), Mitsubishi's iMiEV, and Myers Morto NmG (no more gas). What a wonderful wheeled world awaits us.

Haven't Yet Read Anything that Suits Your Fancy?

About a quarter of U.S. vehicles are SUVs, and they guzzle 33 percent more gas per mile than does the average non-SUV. Try to shift out of an SUV and into a more fuel-efficient car. It can be tough, and I feel your pain. When judgment day came, I couldn't afford a hybrid SUV, but I still clung to big-car specs. My new ride? A five-year-old station wagon. Potentially demoralizing to a cowgirl Mama who drove Jeeps and SUVs — except that it was a Mercedes-Benz for a third less than a hybrid SUV. Not a bad way to sustain our reserves as well as the earth's.

Have you ever dreamed of saying, "I have to run a few errands on my scooter to reduce our carbon footprint"? Scoot(er) back to your child-free days and swap some rolled-up-windshield time for the open air. Opt for an electric variety like the Vectrix to amp up green street cred.

A "Get Out of Jail (Almost) Free!" Card

For a last-chance scenario, consider TerraPass. TerraPass converts your car make and your annual mileage into recommended carbon credit levels. TerraPass also has flight, vacation, and even wedding travel adjustments available. Remember, if you offset vehicle emissions through TerraPass, you can deduct your car or air travel from any other general carbon footprint calculations. Go to *www.Terra Pass.com* to learn more.

> "Restore human legs as a means of travel. Pedestrians rely on food for fuel and need no special parking facilities."
>
> —Lewis Mumford

8

SUSTAINABILITY AT WORK

> "What work I have done I have done because it has been play. If it had been work I shouldn't have done it."
> —Mark Twain

As much as our home is where our hearts are, many times our office is where our time is. Luckily you can apply local living and sustainability principles to any work environment. If you're really lucky, you can make the case to work from home to build the ultimate local life work plan. If you're hankering for a new lease on work life, check out tip two and ten to find sustainability-focused business partners, locally located workplaces or shiny, brand-new earthloving job options.

EYE OPENERS
- Stay home! Americans waste 3.5 billion hours and 5.6 billion gallons of gas sitting in traffic each year.
- Ninety percent of print and writing paper comes from virgin trees. This tree use consumes half of all logged trees.
- If Americans got on the Do Not Mail list *at work as well at home*, we'd save 60 million trees. See *www.dmaconsumers .org/cgi/offmailinglist.*

THE LOCAL LIFE GUIDELINES—YOUR WORK

1. *Stay local:* Telecommute, carpool, walk, bike, or drive a hybrid.
2. *Looking for local work?* Find local and sustainable earth-focused jobs through websites listed in the following section. You also could create a local barter plan.
3. *Cowork:* Share an office.
4. *Save your trees:* Recycle paper, go double-sided, err to electronic vs. paper communiqué, and erase yourself from all mailings of the snail and e-mail varieties.

The Sustainability Screen at Work

Change the World

1. Start Here!

Stay local—telecommute

Cowork—office share

Go paperless

Recycle office supplies and paper

Use at-the-source power strips

Change the lights

Swap the water cooler and bottled water for a tap-water filter

3. Reach For It!

When it's time for new office furniture, upgrade to the eco-friendly models

Choose Energy Star electronics and gear

Team up with a sustainability-oriented partner

IMPACT

2. Why Not?

Bring your own mug

Stock sustainable supplies as well as materials made from recycled products

Practice sustainable processes

4. Save for Last!

Leap to a local job

Start your own locally owned, sustainable business

Baby Steps Count

Simple   **EASE TO DO**   Disruptive

5. *Save your energy:* Look for Energy Star versions of your favorite gear. Most manufacturers have an option, and if they don't, send them the message to get on it.

6. *Power down:* Think sleep modes, at-the-source auto shutoff power cords, rechargeable batteries, and renewable gadget chargers.

7. *Green home turf at work too:* Clean up your lights and set up a complete recycling system.

8. *Sustainable stock:* Skip rubber bands; add in products made from recycled goods—they're everywhere: sticky notes, paperclips, staplers, scissors, folders, tape, even correction fluid (for whoever still uses it). Office Depot and Staples have what you need.

9. *Snack without a trace:* Bring your mugs, skip stirrers, go big on condiments, and gather around the water . . . *filter.*

10. *Partner with sustainable providers:* Choose from eco-friendly Internet, telephone, and hosting services.

The Nitty Gritty: Your Work

Carve out some space on your to-do list to craft a more sustainable work style. Start with where you work and what you do and then expand your sustainability screen to cover everything from electronics and business partners to supplies and snack time.

Stay home!—Telecommuting and Coworking

Wondering how we can save 23 billion gallons of gas each year? Telecommute! In the United States, more than 40 million people work from home some part of each week. Save on commute time and energy waste as well as a few dry-cleaning bills. For help in making your telecommuting case to the boss-woman, check out *www.quint careers.com.* The site details talking points including supporting data

to convert the most staunch cubicle-time bosses to local life work-at-home believers.

FLASHBACK: BARTER DAYS

Consider adding barter to your work repertoire. In addition to earning goods and services through your own labors, you'll add to your local network and neighborhood crew. Don't think you have any skills to barter? Survey your hobbies as well as some of the daily chores you take for granted. Someone whose services you need might be happy to barter for prepared meals (just double a dinner batch), yard work, or weekly shopping, which you can do along with your own.

As you ramp up your talent exchange, consider a barter currency organization such as the FERNIE exchange network. The site organizes talent across geographies and expertise, enabling participants to post a skill and a dollar value per hour. This value is traded via FERNS (Fernie Exchange Resource Network System). As you need a service, you search by skill and community and set up an exchange of your talent for another's based on the FERN value. Visit *www.localcurrency.ca* to learn more.

Looking for New Work? Find a Local and Sustainable Gig

Check out the organizations in the section on *Global Resources for Local Expertise* for some of the eco-leaders. You can also find job postings on these sites:

- *www.Grist.org*
- *www.SustainableBusiness.com/jobs*
- *www.Greenjobs.com*
- *www.IdeaList.org*—for the nonprofit sector

- *www.NetImpact.org*—an MBA network
- *www.treehugger.com*—the Big Daddy Green across Mama Earth

If you're thinking of jumping into the world of small business or entrepreneurship, review the Business Alliance for Local Living Economies (BALLE). BALLE aggregates companies, developments, funders, and community leadership focused on local living to create a networked local living economy. The organization focuses as much on traditional business metrics and stakeholder returns as on local living principles. BALLE offers access to exciting community networks, an infrastructure to create your own, a series of educational conferences and workshops, and economic consulting services. Visit *www.livingeconomies.org* to learn more.

Coworking: Share Office Space

Coworking takes the coziness and vibe of your neighborhood coffee shop and amps up its efficiency with infrastructure. You get to enjoy the community feel of coworkers while leveraging the network and expertise of a larger facility. Office in your 'hood and you can't help but extend your reach into your local community business network. What better way to populate your five-mile (or smaller) driving hub than by knowing the owners of those neighborhood business? And, by sharing one larger roof, you spread energy and water costs across a broader base. That's a local life and sustainability win in one shot.

For an inspiring example, check out Julie Duryea's *www.soukllc .com* in Portland, Oregon. Other city options exist, though they vary in feel and community, so you may want to visit a few. Search for locations near you on *www.coworking.pbwiki.com*.

Sustain: Save Your Trees

Use recycled paper and make double-sided copies. You can find recycled paper at most office supply stores. Look for two things: processed chlorine free (PCF) and high post-consumer waste (PCW) content. Try Grays Harbor Paper 100 or Aspen 100. To print double-sided, print odd pages first, then even (look up how-to in your printer's print options and help sections). Stack paper to recycle in a box or in a binder to avoid crumpling corners, which can create paper jams.

Send Your Paper to School

If you find you have an overflow of recycled paper, donate it to a local school. With the sadly all-too-frequent budget cuts in the public school system, many teachers and school administrators are short on paper and literally can't give the kiddos their assignments. Pull out any confidential materials from the recycled stacks, pack up a few reams, and make a heartwarming field trip to hand-deliver paper to a needy bunch.

Use a paper shredder for nonrecyclables—it's quicker and takes less energy to recycle the shreds. Skip the fax—just scan and e-mail.

Reduce mail *and* e-mail. Get off the mailing lists—at home and at work. Though e-mail saves paper, it's not a sustainability miracle. Somewhere there's a server farm that's chugging through energy to house your data. So, get lean on your virtual mail load too.

Source Sustainable Electronics

As our weekly newspaper's inserts advertise, technology changes in a nanosecond, seemingly requiring us to update gear every Monday morning. Fight the urge and keep a few rules of thumb in mind. Use the sources reviewed in this section to stay current on the hottest gadgets. For an annual comprehensive list and reviews, read Greenpeace

International's "Guide to Greener Electronics," updated quarterly (*www.greenpeace.org*).

SAVINGS SPOTLIGHT: TRY TO SELL E-WASTE FIRST

As you graduate from one e-generation to the next, think cash before trash. Check out sites such as *www.gazelle.com*, *www.cashforlaptops.com*, or *www.sellmyelectronics.com*. You can log on, find your gadget, and find an estimated resale value. Gazelle.com even sends you a prepaid postage box to collect your gadgets. They then resell your toys or recycle them for you. You earn cash and a clean conscience at the same time.

Computers

Use a laptop versus desktop to save *half* the energy (if we all switched it would save $2.5 billion in energy costs). Most manufacturers have Energy Star options for laptop and desktop needs. Apple, Dell, and others are offering mercury-free laptops. And, when you can, opt for LCD screens—they're more energy efficient than plasma.

To find a new computer's rank in eco-friendliness, check out the EPA's ranking database of sixty models at *www.epeat.net*.

Greenpeace gives kudos to Dell, Lenovo, Sony, and Toshiba for their products' recyclability and to Apple, Fujitsu, and HP for eco-manufacturing improvements. *PC Magazine* also does an annual review of computers ranked by eco-friendliness.

Can You Hear Me Now?

For landline phones, go retro and use a cord. Cordless phones eat batteries and suck on power even when they're not in use. Also, lose the headset—they burn battery power. Choose RoHS-compliant devices, especially PDAs. RoHS means your electronics don't have any of the six hazardous materials banned by the 2003 E.U. directive. Most major brands meet the criteria, but ask to be sure.

Save Power

Use your standby and sleep modes on your copier, computer, printer, and fax machines, but take it an extra step with an at-the-source shutoff power strip. You can either set your surge protector power strip to sleep mode or buy one that auto regulates for you. Try Smart Strip Power Strips or The Wattstopper IDP-3050 Plug Load Control Strips. Get surge protection and power savings in one strip.

→ Mom to Mom: ←
E-waste Block Party

If you can't sell your e-waste, consider adding an e-waste collection (and one for hazardous waste as well) into your block party rummage sale. Knowing that a neighborhood, school, or church collection can be piggybacked motivates many a neighbor to purge the junk drawers, closets, and garage hideaways of ripe-for-recycling items. Post the when, where, and how in local coffee shops, grocers, gas stations, and dry cleaners. Empty out your trunk and let the collecting ensue.

Swap disposable batteries for rechargeable options. Try USB cell batteries that charge through your computer's USB port. Extra step: recharge with a solar or wind powered charger. Visit *www.HYmini.com*, *www.Solio.com*, and *www.Batterystuff.com* for a wide selection.

For help with managing and offsetting energy use at the office, check out *www.dsireusa.org*, where you'll find renewable energy sources, a renewable energy credits (REC) database, and potential tax credits.

Recycling: Not Just for Home Anymore

Revisit page 11 for home recycling how-to's that are applicable at work, too. Looking for office-specific gear to go? For office electronics, try *www.wirelessrecycling.com, www.charitablerecycling.com*, or *www.ntrp.org*.

Here are a few more ideas for making work feel like home.

When it's time to replace light bulbs or fixtures, remember your CFLs and LEDs.

Recycle your ink cartridges. Many printer and toner companies do this for you when you reorder (Hewlett-Packard is an example). If yours does not, try *www.aaaenvironmentalinc.com* and *www.tonerbuyer.com.* Better yet, if a major office supply store falls within your drive radius, you can bring cartridges there as most now accept toner cartridges for recycling.

Recycle packing peanuts through LooseFillPackaging.com—or better yet—the Peanut Hotline, 1-800-828-2214. Call with your Zip Code, and the hotline will provide the closest recycling locations. If they can set up a hotline, we can recycle the nuts.

Sustainable Stock

Keep your local screen top of mind and haunt local office supply stores, shipping centers, and mailing locations for supplies. You may even find local manufacturers through your *www.local.com* and Google Maps five-mile-hub exercises. Once you know your local "where," focus on the sustainable "what" via the following list.

Go for refillable pens and pencils—bonus points for those that use recycled materials. You can find them at *www.ecopens.com*.

Ditch the rubber—seventy-five percent of rubber bands come from synthetic oil.

Check out sustainable versions of your longtime favorites. Your local office supply stores now carry most of the basics in sustainable versions. You also can try specialty websites such as *www.sustainable group.com* and *www.greenearthofficesupply.com.*

Snack Without a Trace

Need that three o'clock pick-me-up cup of joe? Use mugs. You can use one 3,000 times versus the—um—one time you use your disposable cup. Find eco-themed mugs at *www.cafepress.com*, corn-made and recycled materials mugs at *www.eco-products.com*, and unique green mugs at *www.uncommongoods.com.*

Skip the stirrers—we toss out 138 billion of them each year. Just put your sugar and milk in the mug first. Your coffee or tea pour will do the rest. And speaking of sugar, go big—use the larger containers of sugar versus single packs.

Lead the (water) way—install a filter in the kitchen sink. There will be plenty of room to gather around for chatter and no water cooler waste to guilt your conscience. See Best Bets For Food and Drink in Chapter 3 for recommendations.

Partner with Sustainability-Oriented Providers

Align your sustainability-minded workplace with like-minded providers. For calling services try these:

Better World Telecom: three percent of all business call revenue goes to nonprofits.

CA Affinity: they offer calling cards with a percentage of transactions donated to sustainable causes.

Credo Mobile: one percent of your charges goes to cause-based nonprofits.

Earth Tones (telephone services): donates profits to eco-causes.

Working Assets: sets up your phone services while donating to eco, peace, and civil rights causes.

For Internet service providers:

Earth Tones: provides web hosting and more, and 100 percent of profits go to eco-orgs.
EcoISP: 50 percent of profits go to your favorite green cause.
Makana Technologies: a piece of your monthly bill goes to green causes.
Affordable Internet Services Online: operates from 100 percent solar powered facilities.

Need a credit card processor? Try Dharma Merchant Services.

Spotlight: Portland's souk: Coworking with Style

Ready to dial back in-office time or dial up out-of-home office space? Coworking may be your answer. Coworking combines the best of coffee-shop community and living-room comfort with hard-core office infrastructure. Whether you're ready to launch a more sustainable business or just want to cut commute times, coworking offers a sustainable life and earth path via shared bandwidth, conference rooms, and office mates' lessons learned.

If you're lucky enough to live near Portland's souk (in Old Town; *www.soukllc.com*), take a tour and settle in. The company's name, souk, means an open air market which embodies the open work space encouraging shared trade and ideas souk offers. The rest of us can learn more about coworking from souk's founder and operator, Julie Duryea. Julie parlayed a lifelong habit of inventive do-gooder-ness (see her bio below) into a successful, local-life focused, sustainability-oriented start-up. And, as a new Mom, Julie is excited to offer other moms an easy way to support work, family flexibility, and eco-living.

What is souk?

Souk provides hourly, daily, and monthly workspace for freelancers, consultants, and entrepreneurs. Our mission is to provide support—beyond just equipped, plug 'n' play, creative office space—to those trailblazing sole proprietors and small businesses (fewer than five employees) in the form of networking events, educational events, and connections to the broader small business support network in Portland.

Since opening in January 2007, these coworking spaces have popped up all over the world.

What motivated you to start a coworking business?

I had so much personal experience working on consulting projects from home, where it was too isolating or I was prey to procrastination with a myriad of other to-do's. I craved a way to have some separation of work and life, but needed a credible office infrastructure. Coffee shops as meeting space often struck me as terribly inappropriate from the standpoint of having your business taken seriously (by you, as well as others). And, of course, a coffee shop's layout is fundamentally not made for meetings.

How does coworking do our planet good?

By sharing power, supplies, and facilities, we help cut back on wasted resources. Coworking helps even from the perspective of better utilizing building space—as we can help fill up underutilized buildings, we delay the need for new office construction. We also set up our facilities to be as sustainable as possible with recycled materials for supplies, auto power down / shutoff modes on electronics, and avid recycling. And, many of our clients come to a coworking solution in order to work closer to their homes, so we cut back on the dreaded car commute footprint.

How were you first inspired to make bettering our environment a priority?

When I was in college at University of California Santa Barbara I'd walk the beach and have to hopscotch oil and tar patches. It was so disheartening to see this epic wide-open beauty scarred by our own sloppiness and waste. Rebuilding a livable earth became even more important to me as I was pregnant with our first baby. We all want our babes to be able to play outside, walk barefoot across the grass—or beach—and be able to share their world with their grandchildren.

To find a co-working space near you, Julie recommends searching *http://coworking.pbwiki.com.*

"Modern technology owes ecology an apology."

—Alan M. Eddison

9

STAYING LEAN: GOOD FOR YOU AND YOUR COMMUNITY

> "Exercise: you don't have time not to."
> —Author Unknown

A commitment to sustainability starts with your own self. As you prioritize an ever-growing list of things to do to build your more locally centered, sustainable life, keep your and your family's health and fitness plan highest on the list. Approaching your day to day with the energy and longevity regular fitness fuels sets you up with the best set of options, decisions, and opportunities. Also, engaging in a hearty dose of athletic play with your neighbors reinforces the community and lifestyle you all are striving to create.

Learn how to incorporate local living (even at the gym), what sustainable gear to wear, and how to meet other environmental warriors (even the weekend variety).

THE LOCAL LIFE GUIDELINES

1. *Go outside:* Burn your energy (calories) instead of Mama Earth's.
2. *Play green:* Join green groups
3. *Go sustainable at your local gym:* Save energy, water, and time.
4. *Recycle gear:* And gear-up recycled at the same time.

The Sustainability Screen: Your Sweat

Change
the World

1. Start Here!

Get out of the gym—play outside!

Bring your own water in a reusable bottle

Use the elliptical or bike before the StairStepper and treadmill

Bring your own towels to the gym

Shorten showers and turn off saunas/steam rooms

Recycle all of your exercise gear

Buy gear made of recycled materials

3. Reach For It!

Take up an outdoor sport

Buy used gear from rental shops, online, and Play It Again stores

Seek out sustainable gyms

IMPACT

2. Why Not?

Start a neighborhood family sport (kickball anyone?)

Maintain your gear to extend its life

Try Ziolite to make clothes last longer

Swim in salt water or ionized pool instead of chlorinated water

Ask your gym to add eco-friendly practices

4. Save for Last!

Vow to be a strictly outdoors family

Power your gear from solar and wind powered sources

Make your own gear from recycled materials

Baby Steps
Count

Simple   **EASE TO DO**   Disruptive

The Nitty Gritty: Your Sweat

Here's some great news: Your community wins and your life improves just by your being in shape.

Scientists estimate the biggest positive sustainability impact of being physically fit comes from avoided medical costs. The benefits of skipping health care costs (think of all the medicines manufactured, packaged, and distributed, never mind the environmental impact of hospitals) outweigh saved CO_2 emissions, gym energy use, and/or the effects of not-so-earth-friendly gear.

So, don't sweat whether or not your every workout saves the earth. Just get out there, get active, and *try* to get local.

Go Outside

Obvious, but still the best local option: get outside for your workouts. Skip the energy, water, and waste generated by gyms and the like in maintaining their facilities for indoor sweats. As an added benefit, you get out and about on the earth you're saving. Shift your family's focus outside by putting one outdoor play event on the weekly calendar. See the following for ideas on what, where, and how.

Keep a few local life tips in mind as you play outside. First, stay on your feet. This may seem obvious, but here's a reminder all the same: minimize driving and flying to outside play. Were you planning on flying to the Boston Marathon from Los Angeles? Support your local fundraiser runs instead. Volunteer or organize hiking trail and ocean cleanups in your community to clean up your tracks. When you need to power up, turn to the extra reusable bottles you keep in stock and sample a few organic fuel feasts.

A Well-Fueled Workout

You'll delight your workout mates (as well as your belly) with this tasty homemade granola recipe from Charmian Christie. This treat is simple, fast, and easily sourced with local ingredients. Visit *www.christiescorner.com* for more delicious, organic, and sometimes vegan or gluten-free recipes. (This recipe is gluten-free if you buy oats marked gluten-free. Many commercial oats contain gluten from cross-contamination during processing.)

INGREDIENTS

- 4 cups rolled oats (do not use quick-cooking or instant)
- 1 cup chopped walnuts (you can use any nut you like, but I'm a walnut fan and it goes well with maple)
- 1 cup pumpkin seeds
- 1 cup flaxseeds (or sesame seeds)
- 1 teaspoon cinnamon
- 1 teaspoon vanilla extract
- ½ teaspoon salt
- ¾ cup dark maple syrup
- 2 cups flaked unsweetened coconut (large flakes are best)
- 2 cups Thompson or Flame raisins

INSTRUCTIONS

1. Preheat oven to 325°F.
2. Combine oats, nuts, and seeds.
3. Mix cinnamon, vanilla, and salt into the maple syrup. Pour maple syrup mixture over the oat mixture and stir well to evenly coat.
4. Spread granola on a cookie sheet and bake for 30 minutes, stirring occasionally.
5. In the meantime, toast the coconut on the stovetop over medium heat in a dry frying pan. The flaked coconut burns very quickly; this method ensures more even cooking.

6. When the granola is golden brown, remove the pan from the oven and empty into a large bowl.

7. Toss the hot granola with the toasted coconut flakes and raisins.

8. When cool, store in an airtight container.

If you barely have enough energy to make your workout, never mind homemade fuel, visit your local food co-op or farmers' market for a locally sourced variety. Remember *www.eatwellguide.org* for sources.

→ **Mom to Mom:** ←
Group Play

Despite wanting to set the best example for kids, busy lives tend to squeeze workouts off the daily plan. In addition to sustaining your energy, sanity, and waistline, it turns out that exercise sustains the planet. So, set an example and bond with other families by working out with your neighbors.

If you're a mom of a baby or toddler, join Mom and Me fitness and yoga classes. Try Baby Boot Camp (*www.babybootcamp.com*), Stroller Strides (*www.strollerstrides.com*), your local yoga studio, and community centers for organized classes. Mom of a school-age child? Make your own team play by setting up a weekly neighborhood soccer game, hike, or bike ride. My friend Aileen inspired great sweat, play, and grins when she organized a regular family kickball night. My husband's family celebrates Thanksgiving in Seattle with an annual neighborhood "Mud Bowl" soccer game, trained for year-round. After sloshing about the field with more than forty people from ages five to seventy-five, you know you've earned your feast!

Corral your favorite playmates plus a few more neighbors you've meant to meet, and let the games begin.

Finding the Great Outdoors

Sometimes the toughest part of outdoor play is finding where to go. Try the following websites for local trails, groups, and rental resources. Checking these sites will let you spend more time sweating the play, and less time sweating the details:

- Hiking—*www.trails.com*, *www.localhikes.com*, *www.trail database.com*
- Outdoor boot camps—The Great Outdoors reviews boot camps on its site (*www.greatoutdoors.com*). You also can look by your location on *www.bootcamp.com*, *www.boot campfinder.com*, or search your web browser for boot camps near you. If you're heading a wee bit north, try *www.Fitness BootcampsCanada.com*
- Running—*www.nikerunning.com*, *www.runtheplanet .com*, *www.usatf.org/routes/search*. Check *Runner's World* magazine for the top ten eco-friendly races at *www.runners world.com/article/0,7120,s6-240-488--12876-0,00.html*
- Walking—*www.traildatabase.com*, *www.walkscore.com* (ranks more than 2,500 neighborhoods for great walking)
- Bicycling—*www.trails.com*, *www.adventurecycling.org/ routes/network.cfm*
- Canoeing/kayaking/rafting—*www.paddling.net*, *www.kayak guide.com*
- Camping—*www.campsites411.com*, *www.reserveamerica .com*, *www.campingsites.com*
- Golf—*www.golfandenvironment.org*
- Sailing—*www.marinasailing.com/FTPRoot/SailingCourses/ classfr.html*

- Skiing—*www.nsaa.org/nsaa/environment/the_greenroom*, *www.skiareacitizens.com* (see Chapter 10 for more eco-friendly ski details)
- Surfing—*www.greensurfers.org*, *www.surfriderfoundation.org* (see Chapter 10 for more eco-friendly surf details)

ADD TO YOUR FAMILY: ADOPT A TRAIL

One way to add a sense of commitment and continuity to your family local life efforts is to "adopt" a specific trail or patch of land. Through our local community projects group, our family has adopted a stretch of beach. Between organized cleanups, we enjoy what we refer to as "our" beach, informally picking up what we can at the end of each day's play. Three times a year we join other families to scour for recyclables and trash. If your locale doesn't have a formal "adopt-a-patch of something" program, start one! Find a trail, beach, or park near you through your state and federal park websites. Visit *www.nps.gov* to find national parks; search your state park department's site for contact information; or try *www.trails4all.org*.

Local Life Groups

Get sustainability momentum going via signing up your family to participate in earth-friendly programs and/or sample local products. Start with the Global Forum for Sports Entertainment (G for SE), which offers a database of sports organizations and venues with reviews on environmental action each group pursues (*www.G-forSE.com*). Continue your search at *www.OrganicAthlete.com*. Organic Athlete is a national organization with many local chapters in the United States and Europe. Organic Athlete organizes athletic events with a sustainability theme and plenty of local eco-info. To suit up in sustainable threads, check out Fair Trade Sports (*www*

.fairtradesports.com). They carry cool, cause-branded gear including Frisbees, hats, shirts, and loads of balls: footballs, basketballs, and soccer balls.

Stay Sustainable at the Gym

When your backyard's great outdoors doesn't seem so welcoming and you decide to head to the gym, you can still make sustainable workout choices. Start by saving water: bring yours and turn off theirs. The water cooler's a sneaky waster. It takes four ounces of water to make the three ounces you drink. And, it's easy to see the waste in filling plastic bottles or tossing disposable cups. Shorten showers; shut off saunas and steam rooms. Even if the gym has an auto cutoff switch, it usually takes longer to turn off the water or steam than if you simply turn it off upon exit. Bring your own towel for drying off. You'll save the water, harsh chemicals, and energy a gym uses to generate the clean "white" towels. When you bring your own you may even feel comfortable using it a second time before tossing it in the wash.

Next, save energy. Step off externally fuel-powered workouts and into your own internally powered sweat steps. Try non-machine workouts like yoga, dance, or weight-bearing exercise to save on the electricity used by machines. If you need to use a machine for variety or low-impact cardio, choose the elliptical or bike over the treadmill and StairMaster. Or power the machine yourself (see Green Gym sidebar below). The average person generates 300 watts of electricity during an hour-long workout—enough power to fuel a television for an hour as well!

Get sustainable and local with a body-and-soul two-for-one, by signing up for a Green Gym. Joining a Green Gym allows you to get some exercise with a group outdoors, often working on projects that make your community a better place. The Green Gym concept started in Britain and is just making its way through the United States. To find or start one, go to *www2.btcv.org.uk/display/greengym.*

Last, you can ask your local gym if it is shifting to a sustainability focus. Many gyms are working hard to reflect eco-friendly practices in their workout and facility operations. Find a gym that's doing some of the following:

- Recycling
- Conserving energy
- Avoiding toxins in their cleaners and their pool
- Reinforcing the recycled products market
- Swapping gym and locker room lights to CFL or LEDs

Recycling for the Home Team

As in all areas of your local life, repurposing your athletic gear and clothes delivers a sustainability win. Give your gear a long life by maintaining what you've got. When it's time to let it live anew, put your community networks to work. Try Freecyling and your local Play It Again store for sport-specific swaps. If you live in a mountain town, give SWAG (Sharing Warmth Around the Globe) a try to repurpose snow equipment. And don't forget to augment the neighborhood rummage sale with season-specific swaps to outfit your community's kids in age-appropriate gently used gear.

> "I think that anyone who comes upon a Nautilus machine suddenly will agree with me that its prototype was clearly invented at some time in history when torture was considered a reasonable alternative to diplomacy."
>
> —Anna Quindlen

FAMILY PLAY TIME:
LOCAL LEISURE

"Happiness consists of living each day as if it were the first day of your honeymoon and the last day of your vacation."

—Anonymous

Here's a sad, scary, and sorry stat: a recent study found that a third of employees don't use paid vacation time. Rationale for wasting this resource included getting behind at work and not being able to afford the trip. For the first "reason," I say that only a mighty few of us work in professions where our day-to-day presence truly ensures the life and safety of our peers. The majority of us can put the work aside. Really, we can. As for the second reason, peruse the tips in that chapter to put that excuse to rest as well. Vacation on, mighty warriors!

YOUR LOCAL LIFE GUIDELINES
1. *Staycation like a pro:* Set ground rules, expand the playbook, and relish less stress.
2. *Must travel? Remember sustainability tips:* Be a green hotel guest. Minimize air travel and try buying carbon credits. Ride lightly. And, keep hometown sustainability style on the road.
3. *Visit sustainable playgrounds:* Try earth-loving locales and volunteer vacations.

The Nitty Gritty: Your Play

Vacation time should be stress- (and relatively) guilt-free. Peruse the how-tos below to pick the few that feel achievable and energizing during your time away from the day-to-day. You'll note how familiar many of them now feel, so give yourself credit for keeping the simple local-life guidelines in play while you do the same.

The Sustainability Screen: Good Times

Change the World

1. Start Here!

Amp up your staycation prowess

Search out sustainable lodging and keep your sustainability screen in place

Check out the town with your feet or two wheels instead of four

Must drive? Choose alternate energy options

Calculate and offset your carbon credits

3. Reach For It!

Try sustainability-oriented adventures like eco-resorts, volunteer vacations, and rafting, biking, or hiking trips

Consume less on the road—pack your meals and leave trinkets behind

Donate to eco-causes in your destination

IMPACT

2. Why Not?

Leave your house in sustainability mode: time lights and water; stop mail and papers

Go paperless—use e-tickets, itineraries, maps, etc.

Recycle guide books

Support locally owned business and resources in your destination

4. Save for Last!

Consider a volunteer vacation

Get to your vacation without fossil fuels used in air, car, and powerboat travel

Find local crops for your feasts rather than dining out

Baby Steps Count

Simple   **EASE TO DO**   Disruptive

Staycation, All You Ever Wanted 🏷

Here's an obvious—and surprisingly energizing—trend to factor into your local life game plan: the staycation. Economic conditions aside, the staycation introduces you to your local terrain in a way your daily routine can never aspire to do. As steeped as you may already be in staycation ideas, peruse the following tips to amp up your local leisure.

Set the Tone and Hold the Line

Have a family powwow at least a month in advance to make sure everyone understands the ground rules: no work, no chores, no (or very, very few) weekly routine activities. Before you plot and scheme activity one, clear the books, hide the electronics, swear off home chores (consider bringing in home help if you can't live with piles of dirty dishes and laundry—see the Chores No More sidebar) and bury alarm clocks. Really, how many vacations do you spend washing your car, running errands, or doing heaps of dishes and laundry?

CHORES NO MORE

If hiring home help creates more stress than a staycation can release, consider setting up a home help trade. Check in with friends and neighbors who are most likely navigating similar economic conditions. Even if they're not heading out (or in) for an escape any time soon, they may be interested in a break from the weekly cleaning routine or may value a set of chores that you (or better yet, your kids) may be able to do on their behalf.

No free labor? Check with neighborhood kids. All you really need is enough help to make sure you're not distracted from your staycation goals: relax and recharge. Cheap—albeit inexperienced—help can fit the bill.

Invite everyone to prepare local "tour guidebooks." If you don't live in an obvious tourist attraction locale, get online for research, talk to your local chamber of commerce, visit the library, or check with large local hotels for a list of your town's "things to do." You will—without a doubt—be amazed at what there is to do with true leisure time in your own backyard. Depending on family dynamics and kids' ages, you may also want to set an expectation around how much of your staycation time is spent together versus time spent individually refueling your tanks.

Think Outside the Guide

You've worked the museums, water parks, balloon rides, outdoor trails, and performing arts lists. Once you've mined the local tourist info, survey your crew for interest in some off-the-path adventures. Consider sustainability-oriented options such as touring your local landfill or recycling facilities. Review your list of local businesses and set up a tour of any manufacturing facilities or local operations appealing to your crew. Find a hands-on tour of a local farm or CSA. Take a local-eats cooking class or do-it-yourself repair workshop. If such "mundane" locales don't ignite enthusiasm, pick one to champion and trade it for a more obvious fun-friendly adventure. Your kids may be amazed at how cool it is to see how something they eat or use every day actually comes to be. Trigger that interest and then you can slot a few more spots like these into the itinerary.

Once you've set your plan, settle in to reap the rewards of no airport stress, no lodging costs, and a new perspective on treasures close to home.

Savings Sources

As you plot your great at-home getaway, take advantage of a few tools to help manage costs so you can spend more on play and less on logistics. For activities and entertainment, consider buying a local savings book such as those found at *www.entertainment.com* and *www.citypass.com.* If you find a place that's a huge family hit, consider buying an annual pass. A few visits on your staycation alone may hit the break-even level.

GLOBAL GETAWAYS AT HOME

As compelling as the staycation continues to be, you may lament the loss of perspective that traveling to unknown locales provides. Create an at-home world tour by weaving global themes into your plan. Choose an area of the world to "visit" each day. Sample Indian food, see a Bollywood flick, and take a family yoga class one day. Hold a pizza taste-test, visit the opera, and play bocci ball the next. Mix in a *chili con queso* cook-off, a salsa dancing class, and a family or neighborhood soccer tournament another day. You get the idea. Create your own family's global themes—geographies, languages, arts—even poetry—and craft your staycation around them.

Want to amp up the global fare? Consider bringing a global traveler to stay in your home during your staycation. He or she will appreciate the home stay, value a preplanned itinerary, bring a new lens to your local turf, and sprinkle a bit of world flavor amongst your family. Check out *www.exchangetravelers.com, www.couchsurfing .org,* or *www.hospitalityclub.org.* Or, explore your kids' school for partnership student exchanges.

To manage gas costs, try the AAA gas mileage calculator at *www .aaafuelcostcalculator.com* to figure out your fuel needs, and sites like *www.gasbuddy.com* or Google Maps to find the cheapest gas near you. If one of your staycation ideas requires an overnight stay nearby, consider a home exchange. Sites like HomeExchange.com, HomeSwap.com, or InterVacaUS.com facilitate trades.

Sustainable Travel on the Road

Even if you venture outside your local radius, you can minimize your travel footprint with a little up-front planning. Between sustainable travel practices, eco-lodging and tours, and volunteer vacations, you can convert your decadent sojourner selves into sustainability saints. For the undeniably unsustainable arenas you simply cannot overcome (such as traveling by air), repent and mitigate travel sins via carbon offsets.

Be a Green Guest

Lead the sustainability brigade at your family's hotel stay. Pass on the towel changes and room cleaning. Shorten up showers and sink use. And, painful as it is (at least for me), fight the urge to use and take home those fun tiny toiletries. They're packaging monsters, and the more we use the more manufacturers make. Turn off a few lights and turn down the heat (or turn up the AC). Last, keep the minibar closed. Not only do you save the 300 percent markup, but you avoid the little packaging hogs there too.

Plot sustainable stays by selecting earth-friendly hotels. When you're investigating reservations, ask if the hotel participates in The Green Hotel Initiative (see *www.ceres.org* for more details) to ensure that sustainability practices are under way. Or, make it easy and choose one of the hotel chains listed here.

NATIONWIDE HOTELS

- Fairmont Group Hotels (*www.Fairmont.com*)—The Fairmont Hotels implement a wide range of eco-friendly policies, from cleaning and maintenance processes to organic menus and sustainable energy technology.
- InterContinental Hotels (*www.ichotelsgroup.com*)—See the InterContinental sidebar for details.

- Kimpton Hotels (*www.KimptonHotels.com*)—The Kimpton group offers an eclectic collection of "boutique" properties. Sustainability efforts span across all aspects of operations including extensive recycling, eco-friendly cleaning supplies, water and energy conservation programs, and organic food options. Plus, all paper items are made from recycled papers with soy inks.
- Starwood Group (*www.starwoodhotels.com*)—The Starwood Group already has revised many processes, products, and menus to reflect eco-conscious living. In addition to its current portfolio, which includes the Westin, W, and Sheraton hotels, Starwood is soon to open additional properties with a greater emphasis on eco-principles. Look for the Aloft, Element, and #1 hotel brands, which will be sustainability based.

INTERCONTINENTAL HOTELS GROUP (IHG) ENGAGE GREEN WITH "GREEN ENGAGE" SYSTEMS

IHG is the world's largest hotel company (by room count), owning hotel brands including Crowne Plaza, Holiday Inn, InterContinental, and Staybridge Suites. With more than 4,100 hotels and 600,000 rooms, IHG offers a large-scale platform to test sustainability programs. IHG leadership developed the Green Engage program to address energy consumption as a tool to improve both environmental conservation efforts and business performance.

Green Engage allows hotel managers to measure energy and water use, waste production, and carbon emissions. In addition to providing data, the tool offers benchmarks against other IHG hotels to help the managers gauge relative performance. The program also recommends initiatives to impact usage levels and provides a reporting tool to track progress. To learn more or book a stay, visit *www.ichotelsgroup.com*.

As your travel interests and requirements change, use eco-lodging databases to help sort through offerings that meet your sustainability screen. For a roundup of options, check the following databases.

BEST LODGING DATABASES

- *www.roadandtravel.com/bedbreakfast/2007/eco-friendly b&bs.htm*
- *www.environmentallyfriendlyhotels.com*
- *www.ecohotelsoftheworld.com*
- *www.ethicaltraveler.com*
- *www.greenhotels.com*
- *www.greenhotelreviews.com*
- *www.goodtravelcompany.com*
- *www.greentravelhub.com*
- *www.ecotourism.org*
- *www.blog.SustainableTravel.com*
- *www.SustainableTravelInternational.org*

Minimize Air Travel

With more than 2 billion passengers flying each year, it's no wonder air travel contributes almost 100 percent of all nitrogen oxide emissions. As tough as air travel may be on our environment, it's often tougher to get to your adventure without a plane. In order to offset the CO_2 impact, buy carbon credits. You can adjust for travel on your overall carbon credit adjustment efforts or buy travel-specific carbon credits. These are a few to try:

- AtmosFair — offers a CO2 calculator by flight: *www.atmosfair .de/index.php?L=3*
- A Better World Club — *www.betterworldclub.com*
- Native Energy — *www.nativeenergy.com*

- Sustainable Travel International—STI also organizes eco-friendly travel across a myriad of market packages: *www.Sustainable TravelInternational.com*
- TerraPass—*www.TerraPass.com*
- Virgin Air—all profits from air and train business units go to Virgin Fuel, which researches and builds alternate, renewable fuel sources: *www.virginamerica.com*

Ride Lightly

Trained lately? If not, try it. They're sustainable, they're old school, and they're downright sexy. Try a combo train-and-hike itinerary offered via an Amtrak–National Parks Association partnership (*www .nps.gov/findapark/trailsandrails.htm*). Once you've arrived, it's tough to get to know a city any better than by pounding the pavement or cycling the streets. If you just can't make that happen, green rental car options can save the day. Ask for hybrids at the standard players, or support one of the sustainability-focused options from this list:

SUSTAINABLE RENTALS/SHUTTLES
- Biobeetle(California, Hawaii)—*www.biobeetle.com*
- Eco Limo (LA, West Coast)—*www.eco-limo.com*
- OZOcar (East)—*www.ozocar.com*

Or, really get to know the locale and the locals by giving car-sharing a roll. Bold, but guaranteed to help you unveil a few locals-only haunts. Find one in your arrival city via CarSharing.net (flip back to Chapter 7 for more options).

Hometown Sustainability on the Road
Be your daily at-home good earth citizen while on the road. Keep the family local life plan marching forward by cutting back on paper

use. Default to online maps, itineraries, boarding passes, and check-in as well as online updates and hellos (and digital photos) to those left behind. If you need hard copies, try doing all of your research at your local library or via used guidebooks. Of course, remember to recycle any that you buy. 🏷

Once you're ready to head out the door, pack lightly to minimize the carbon costs of carrying your load. Travel during the off-season to save money and lighten the load on Mama Earth. 🏷 When you arrive, live like your local selves by experiencing the heart of a culture: eat locally grown foods. Search the Eat Well Guide (*www.eatwellguide.org/i.php?pd=Home*) for locally sourced cuisine while you're on the road. The guide covers the United States and Canada, with an eye to adding more destinations regularly. Before you lock the door behind you, be sure your home will be energy efficient while you're gone—the AC/heating set higher/lower than normal, lights off or timed if needed for security, paper and mail stopped, water off or on timed cycles. 🏷

Sustainable Playgrounds

Focus vacations around sustainable locales or resorts that support the earth's long march. You can spend your vacation helping a group build out infrastructure to improve environmental conditions. Or, you can simply roam wild, enjoying Mama Earth.

To find your adventure, check out the information that follows. If the list overlooks your favorite play, flip back to Chapter 9 for more outdoor activities.

General Resorts

The following groups maintain a variety of properties and excursions to get your family out to play. In addition to destinations and itineraries, many of the groups offer frequency programs and other incentives to keep your family coming back for more:

- Gap Adventures—*www.gapadventures.com*
- Real Adventures—*www.realadventures.com*
- TIES (The International Ecotourism Society)—*www.eco tourism.org*
- VISIT (Voluntary Initiative for Sustainability in Ecotourism)—*www.visit21.net*

→ **Mom to Mom:** ←
Go While You Still Can

Sad and shocking, but true: many places we know and love (or would love if we knew them) are likely to disappear in our lifetimes, or in our children's. Highlight the importance of your family's sustainability efforts by visiting some of the soon-to-disappear hot spots while you can. For quick reference and a thorough hit list, try *Frommer's 500 Places to See Before They Disappear*. The guide organizes options by geography and topic such as Big Skies, Where History Was Made, and Disposable Culture. To build a short list to try, cross-reference the guide with a book such as *1000 Places to See Before You Die* by Patricia Schultz. Remember to visit them in as sustainable a manner as possible so as not to accelerate their exit: tread softly, leave nothing behind, and buy carbon credits to offset your travel to get there.

Biking Tours

Ever since our good friends Julie and Leslie cycled the Tour de France route (at a pace a wee bit less grueling in order to savor local wines, cuisine, and inns), I hear the call of the bike seat. Now, if only my legs would listen and train up for the adventure. If you're ready to explore great destinations as well as the roads that lead there, try a bike tour. Most operators offer routes for multiple skill levels as well as a backup van to whisk you away should your feet lose the urge to pedal. These operators emphasize eco-friendly principles and routes to keep cyclists in touch with the earth they're riding:

- Backroads—*www.Backroads.com*
- Biking Adventures—*www.BikingAdventures.com*
- Escape Adventures—*www.EscapeAdventures.com*
- Sustainable Energy in Motion Biking Tour—*www.common circle.com*
- Wild Heart Cycling—*www.WildHeartCycling.com*

Golf

With loads of irrigation needs, questionable foliage impacts, and much earth moving required to build a course, golf may seem oddly un-green. However, many course and club operators are working to reduce their carbon footprints. Check the following databases for an updated list of golf groups carving out sustainability-minded courses:

- Audubon Certified Golf Courses—*www.audubon international.org/programs/acss/golf.htm*
- Golf and the Environment—*www.golfandenvironment.org, ecofriendlygolf.htm*

Surfing

Some of the first tree-huggers had their epiphany in the water. It's hard to spend hours in the surf pondering the waves and the beach ahead without also noting the direct effects of oil spills and trash in the water, and the fact that there are fewer surf-able locales. These groups offer ways to get involved with surf care as well as tips on a few somewhat still-hidden gems to surf:

- GreenSurf (*www.greensurf.org*)—Supports eco-efforts, eco-surf locales, green practices, and financial support options.
- Green Surfers (*www.greensurfers.org*)—Surfers advocating a green lifestyle with general tips and how-to's as well as surf-specific recommendations.
- Surfrider Foundation(*www.surfrider.org*)—Dedicated to preserving places to surf; offers tips, legislation overviews, and paths for participation.

Skiing and Boarding

Each year winter athletes and snow resorts lament a tangible impact of global warming: lost ski days. Fortunately this direct effect motivated leaders in winter vacationing to aggressively publicize the need to build, live, and ski in accordance with sustainability choices. Groups like SACA and NSAA (see following list) keep eco-awareness high, while resorts like Aspen and Silverton translate environmental causes into actionable business.

If you can't visit one of the eco-operated leaders, visit *www.Ski Green.org* to buy carbon offsets to your winter play.

- Ski Green—Buy carbon offsets through ski resort minitags. Each tag represents 100 kilowatt hours of wind power. See *www.skigreen.org* for participating resorts.
- Ski Area Citizens Association (SACA)—This is an independent organization ranking all U.S. ski resorts by environmental impact. Check out *www.skiareacitizens.com/index .php?nav=top_ten* for the top ten resorts. The site also lists the worst ten to visit.

- National Ski Area Association (NSAA)—Participates in Keep Winter Cool, and Sustainable Slopes. Both organizations help raise awareness about global warming's impact on mountain terrain as well as develop eco-guidelines for resort locations. Visit *www.nsaa.org*

> **→ Mom to Mom: ←**
> **Bug Off**
>
> To keep pesky pests away, first cover up with hats and long-sleeved shirts and pants. Most repellents—especially the ones made with DEET—contain skin irritants. Some less toxic and more organic options include Smart Shield (sunscreen *and* bug repellent), Bubble and Bee, Skedattle, and Bygone Buzz—made with lemon and eucalyptus oil.

Volunteer Vacations

How about doing good for the planet, your bank account, and your conscience in one trip? Shift gears and try a family volunteer vacation. So many options exist. You can travel the world or stay stateside and sample projects across a broad range of interests:

- Center for Cultural Interchange—*www.cci-exchange.com*
- The Charity Guide—*www.charityguide.org/volunteer/vacations.htm*
- Cross Cultural Solutions—*www.crossculturalsolutions.org*
- Cultural Restoration Tourism Project—*www.crtp.net*
- Earthwatch Institute—*www.earthwatch.org*
- Global Volunteers—*www.GlobalVolunteers.com*
- Habitat for Humanity—*www.habitat.org*

- Operation Cross Roads Africa (exchange)—*www.operation crossroadsafrica.org.*
- Travel with Conscience (higher end cost)—*www.TravelWith Conscience.com*
- Wilderness Volunteers—*www.WildernessVolunteers.com*
- World Wide Opportunities on Organic Farms (WWOOF) program—*www.wwoof.org*
- World Wildlife Fund—*www.worldwildlife.org.*

→ Mom to Mom: ←
Digital Scrapbooking

The good news is that digital cameras turn almost everyone into a professional—or at least inspire us all to keep trying to capture the shot until we're close. The downside: this can mean hundreds more photos to store, sort, and slip into albums. With all of that paper . . . not a sustainability-oriented endeavor. Bypass physical album efforts *and* get sustainable by switching to online photo albums, blogs, family websites, and photo books. Challenge everyone in your family to put together their favorite vacation vignettes. Collect and share with friends and family upon your return. In addition to the online albums and photo printing sites like Shutterfly, Kodak's Snapfish, and Apple's iPhoto line, try *www.digitalscrapbookplace.com* for digital scrapbooks and *www .inkubook.com* for photo books printed on recycled paper.

"Laughter is an instant vacation."

—Milton Berle

SAVING MONEY AND THE EARTH
AT THE SAME TIME

> "When I was young I thought that money was the most important thing in life; now that I am old, I know it is."
>
> —Oscar Wilde

There was a day when "green" clearly translated to "money." And, for most of us, that's still the overridingly important green in our lives. You don't have to throw out financial requirements and goals in order to support a sustainable and local life mantra. To sync your personal sustainability with the earth's longevity, tweak a few practices in your banking and investing life. When the timing is right, you may even consider some cutting-edge sustainable high-tech investments or microfinancing. These resources will help you navigate options.

EYE OPENER
- Switching to online bill pay for all of your accounts saves more than six pounds of paper per home each year.

THE LOCAL LIFE GUIDELINES—YOUR MONEY
1. *Go paperless:* Finally—fully—automate bill pay and banking and skip ATM receipts. Makes life easier for you and cleaner for the earth.

2. *Go local:* Try microfinance—investing in local, small entities to build your community's eco-businesses.
3. *Have a green heart:* Give to eco-causes.
4. *Try sustainability-oriented banks:* Many local and regional banks have reoriented their operations around sustainability

The Sustainability Screen: Your Money

Change the World

1. Start Here!

Spend less

Go paperless with online bill pay and banking

Shift to a sustainability-focused credit card

Align family financial and investment goals to match local life, sustainability-focused plans

Structure children's allowance to reinforce family financial planning

3. Reach For It!

Invest in sustainable assets: indices, funds, companies

Track and invest in local life and sustainability trends

Start a Mama's green giving circle

Switch over your account at a national bank to a smaller institution based in your hometown

IMPACT

2. Why Not?

Invest in locally based businesses and causes

Request checks printed on recycled paper

Donate and volunteer for local causes

Start a Mama's (and families') local, sustainable investment group

4. Save for Last!

Shift your 401(k) to an eco-401(k)

Support small, local businesses

Micro-invest locally

Baby Steps Count

Simple   **EASE TO DO**   Disruptive

initiatives such as reducing paper use, increasing energy efficiency, building eco-certified offices, and funding local green causes.

5. *Focus your credit cards:* Many cards either implement sustainability processes or donate to local eco-causes.

The Nitty Gritty: Your Money

How can you protect and grow your family's money while reinforcing local community initiatives? Consider a myriad of steps from simply saving paper to targeting cutting edge eco-technologies.

Go Paperless

This is an easy and high-impact local life tip: try to automate all of your bills and banking. At a minimum, get your checks printed on recycled paper and skip printing out your ATM receipts. To get online automation in place, you can either go to your bank's website for set-up instructions or try About.com for a good overview (*www.banking.about.com/od/bankonline/f/setupbillpay.htm*). Remember to include any carbon offsets or alternate energy programs on your auto-pay schedule.

Go Local—Support Microlending

The idea of microlending or microfinance hit the global screen with the work of Muhammad Yunus and the Bangladesh-based Grameen Bank. Both Mr. Yunus and Grameen Bank won the Nobel Peace Prize in 2006 for their work in crafting and driving a broad-scale plan to use an economic engine (individual and small business loans) to drive whole-scale societal change. Microlending enables people to get on their feet via small loans—such as $50. In some cases, a locally based business attracts many small loans to build a bigger infrastructure, develop new products, or expand its distribution. In addition to changing the world, this creates a local life and sustainability win by supporting local businesses that service local communities.

You can learn more about microlending by reading the overview on the Community Investing Center website (*www.community investingcenterdb.org*). The site also provides a database where you can look up organizations to review their location, record, and areas of focus. Check *www.forbes.com* for its annual ranking of the world's top fifty microfinance organizations. The updated list tends to come out at the calendar year's end. For a broad menu of causes to support, try *www.kiva.org*. Kiva is the first large network connecting global lenders and borrowers (mostly Third World). The organization provides a breadth of investment opportunities to suit almost any interest or cause. Similarly to Kiva, MicroPlace Visit (*www.microplace.com*) offers global investment opportunities tagged by easy-to-reference screens such as location, estimated return on investment, and poverty level you're impacting. Or, go to where it all started, The Grameen Foundation, which includes a global network of fifty-two microfinance institution (MFI) partners including Growth Guarantee partners. The organization has worked with more than 31 million people in twenty-three countries. Visit *www.grameenfoundation.org*.

If specific geographies or recipients interest you, there are investment vehicles organized around different target groups. For example, Accion has been targeting small loans since 1973 and is active mostly in Latin America and Asia (*www.accion.org*). You can also choose to specifically reach women borrowers. Financial Women's Association sponsors women small business borrowers worldwide; visit *www .fwa.org/community/microfinance.htm* to learn more. Pro Mujer (*www.promujer.org*) targets poor women who lack the education and skills they need to qualify for employment or to access credit. Finally, Women Advancing Microfinance works to support women in the administration of microfinance; *www.wam-international.org*.

MAMMA MICROFINANCE

Keep your eye on your hometown to support small businesses and women in need. Band together with a group of like-minded Mamas to set up a sustainability-focused equity fund. Work with your local Small Business Administration (SBA) office or one of the U.S.-based microfinance organizations to find a green-oriented entrepreneur in your backyard. In our neighborhood, the emagineGreen direct sales business (see the Chapter 6 Spotlight for more details) offers women interested in building their own business around green causes a chance to piggyback on a large company infrastructure. When a friend wanted to become a green coach but didn't have the start-up capital required, we were able to sponsor her. Support a local Mama, grow sustainability, and experience backyard microfinancing: the trifecta!

Have a Green Heart—
Give to Local Eco-friendly Causes

Charity Navigator and Guidestar provide detailed reviews and comparisons on many of nonprofit organizations servicing a breadth of causes. Review eco-friendly causes here to pick your green philanthropy partner: *www.Charitynavigator.org* and *www.Guidestar.org*.

To stay closer to home, create a giving circle with your Mama network. A study by the Forum of Regional Associations of Grantmakers reported that giving circles doubled between 2004 and 2006 and donated more than $100 million during the last four years. Think about the reach and impact you could have on your hometown by organizing a giving circle around a person, family, company, or cause in need. Check out *www.givingforum.org* or *www.givingcircles.org* to learn more.

Sustainable Personal Banking

Local banks or credit unions can incorporate a sustainability focus across operations. First ask about some of the basics. Leading banks have been building various sustainability practices into their operations, such as recycling, ensuring that facilities meet LEED certification, installing efficient lighting, providing incentive for employees to adopt sustainability practices (for example, carpooling or using local transportation), and printing on recycled paper. Any business can put these basics into place. If your bank hasn't done so, call the manager's attention to sustainability principles. Even though many banks feel big and anonymous—and perhaps recently, impersonal—a local bank manager can put many of the sustainability basics in place.

Next, check to see if your bank invests in green entities and developments. Does the bank proactively loan to businesses pursuing sustainability initiatives? Will the bank competitively finance your upgrade efforts at home or at work?

A final way a bank may support a more earth-friendly business approach is through microfinance, which often involves capital support to companies doing work in your backyard. By staying local, businesses can reduce their carbon footprint, which makes all of our backyards a better place.

MAKING MAMMA MOOLA

Swap a book club night for an investment night. Focus a women's investment group on the local life by targeting your picks to local companies or community sustainability initiatives. Once you've hit your stride, consider expanding your group's reach to include kids, using the kids' savings tip in the Seed Money sidebar.

There are some banks that either pursue sustainability business and consumer efforts or offer attractive loan rates to initiatives.

If you're interested in a sustainability-focused bank, review New Resource Bank, Vermont's Chittenden Bank, Santa Fe's Permaculture Credit Union, ShoreBank Pacific, and Wainwright Bank of Boston. Although mainstream banks have come under fire across all operations, a few still support eco-initiatives. Investigate Bank of America, HSBC, and Wells Fargo to test an eco-fit.

SEED MONEY:
ENCOURAGING KIDS TO SAVE THEIR GREEN

Include your kids' savings accounts in your banking plan. On one of my first visits to my in-laws' home, they retrieved a weathered notebook from the kitchen drawer. Crusty and dusty, it told a tale of four kids and twenty-five years of fiscal lessons wrought via hand-calculated interest rates, weekly journal entries, and cross-family loans. The handwriting changed by child, age, and spending urgency, but the basic banking principles remained constant. Red ink—in a decidedly older hand—reworked miscalculated entries, nudging young minds back onto their savings path. The "Bank Book" tells the story of how to earn money, save money and—mindfully—spend money. Moms can use online banking to set up a paperless version of this tool (and download statements for posterity).

Start by allocating allowances into four categories: disposable income, savings, investments, and philanthropic causes (and, of course, a plug here for the causes being environmentally oriented). Determine a mix that matches your family values, and leave the details on which investments and causes deserve the cash to your kids.

Take your family fiscal plan a step further. Connect with a few other families to create a kids' finance community. Use monthly meetings to compare savings account investment ideas and philanthropic groups.

Always check out a bank prior to handing over your assets. Consult a couple of resources regularly to compare and update bank reviews. Visit the National Green Pages (*www.coopamerica.com*), Bankrates.com, and GoTalkMoney.com to get started.

Local Life Credit Cards

First, revisit your mantra of buy none, buy less, buy used and—finally—buy local. Recent economic conditions alone warrant a serious "buy none or buy less" second thought. Fiscal conservation and environmental conservation can be great partners. If you're still buying, ease your spending impact a wee bit with earth-friendly credit cards. Most of these cards mimic affinity or cause-related cards by giving a percentage of the spending to local life causes, and many times these causes include carbon credit offsets. Always double-check to ensure the credit card financing rate competes with mainstream cards. If you want to donate to a local life cause, you can contribute money directly to the organization. You do not need to overpay on credit card fees to do so. As of this book's publication date, all cards in the following list offered market rates for fees and financing charges. However, always check.

Brighter Planet Visa (issued by Bank of America)—The card matches each dollar spent with a reward points. Cardholders can then aggregate points to trade for carbon offsets.

Defenders of Wildlife—the company donates a portion of your spending to habitat conservation.

Earth Rewards MasterCard (issued by General Electric)—The company invests 1 percent of spending in a series of emission-reduction projects.

Green Pay MasterCard (issued by MetaBank)—The card allows users to build up carbon offsets with each purchase.

Salmon Nation Visa (issued by Shorebank)—The bank donates to help fish habitats in the Northwest.

Working Assets Visa Card—The company donates ten cents of every purchase to charities you choose from its list of fifty different causes.

> "A wise man should have money in his
> head, but not in his heart."
>
> —Jonathan Swift

12

GIFT GIVING AND HOLIDAYS:
THE ULTIMATE SUSTAINABILITY CHALLENGE

> "The more you praise and celebrate your life,
> the more there is in life to celebrate."
>
> —Oprah Winfrey

Celebrations often define our family traditions. Reshape your family's rituals to include local and environmental concerns through a few simple sustainability slants. Start by rethinking how much "consumption" a celebration really requires. Most of the good stuff we remember about holiday events centers around time shared and grins traded. As you think about sourcing essential food, décor, and gifts, remember sustainability themes around recycling, finding organic/ local products, and saving energy and water as you bring holiday magic to life. Though the first few celebrations may require more setup or thinking time than usual, you can savor the satisfaction of knowing that *your* kids will pass on sustainability practices as part of *their* "family traditions." This chapter covers most major holidays, birthdays, and a few celebrations for Mama Earth.

EYE OPENERS
- If every American family wrapped just three presents in reused materials, we'd save enough paper to cover 45,000 football

The Sustainability Screen: Your Celebrations

Change the World

IMPACT

Baby Steps Count

Simple   **EASE TO DO**   Disruptive

1. Start Here!

Add Earth Day (April 22) and Recycling Day (November 15) to your annual holiday calendar

Choose recycled or plantable papers for cards and wrapping

Recycle old décor

Choose LED lights and recycle old ones

Use disposable items made from recycled materials or bamboo

3. Reach For It!

Set up birthday gifts to be local-cause donations instead of more "stuff"

Plan an all-organic or local menu for celebrations

Organize a décor and gift swap meet

Swear off disposable serving items

Publicize a family "no 'thing' gifts, please" preference

Choose a Christmas tree you can plant after the holidays

2. Why Not?

Go digital for all greetings

Get creative and swear off gift wrapping unless it's from recycled items

Outfit for Halloween via a costume swap party

Give gifts of time and experiences instead of things

If you celebrate Christmas, choose a sustainably farmed tree

4. Save for Last!

Plan holiday feast menus around homegrown foods

Hand-make all gifts

Skip the Christmas tree

fields. Or, just forgo those presents and save the energy and resources needed to make those gifts as well as the paper!

- Americans eat close to 25 pounds of candy per person each year. (Yikes! That makes Chapter 9 even more important for us.)
- American homes produce 25 percent more trash than usual between Thanksgiving and New Year's Day. It adds up to 25 million *extra* tons of waste.
- Between Thanksgiving and New Year's Day, Americans use 27 percent more energy than the non-holiday periods of the year.

YOUR CELEBRATIONS: THE LOCAL LIFE GUIDELINES

1. Gift—and greet—locally: Less is more.
2. Wrap right (or not at all).
3. Eat green lean (and lean green).
4. Create high-impact magic through low-impact décor.
5. Use holiday cheat sheets to create sustainability-oriented celebrations.

The Nitty Gritty:
The Local Life Guidelines for Your Celebrations

Gift-wrap waste, evil plastic décor, power-taxing lights, and overdone consumption . . . don't let local living awareness damper a Mama's expertise: celebrations! Just adapt your celebratory spirit around a few Local Life Guidelines and plot specific holidays with these tips.

Gift—and Greet—Locally

Thanks to big hearts (and big business), most holidays involve some exchange of good wishes and gifts. You can still revel in shared cheer; just use the tips in this chapter to broaden the list of recipients to include Mama Earth. Buy less, recycle more, and swap gifts of your time and self for gifts off the shelf.

Create Close-to-Your-Heart (and Hearth) Greetings

When possible, digitize your cheer. Better bandwidth means that better graphics, bells, and whistles make it from your computer to friends and family. Spend the time saved skipping a 3D note—no shopping or stamping—to amp up your 2D e-greeting's message. A haiku perhaps? A family picture? (Always!) Try these sites to design your e-card.

- *www.123Greetings.com*
- *www.Buzzle.com*
- *www.StoryPeople.com*

When 2D e-greetings just won't do, stay true by choosing sustainability-oriented cards: recycled paper, recyclable materials, few added decorations, and no plastic. *Tip: look on the back of card to see how much post-consumer paper makes up the card.* Better yet, get crafty and recycle cards received. Often the card front is inscription-free, so you can cut it off and send as a postcard—reduced postage too! Out of time to be crafty? Send cards on to St. Jude's Ranch (*www.stjudes ranch.org*), where the kids will use the fronts to make new cards.

HANDMADE HOLIDAY-GRAMS

You've spent the year digging into your local 'hood. Put your extended community to work and rally neighborhood kids for all-hands card crafting session. Poll the parents to determine how many cards you may need and what themes resonate. Then pool resources and scrap baskets to collect card supplies for an afternoon of creativity, with carols and homemade taste treats for incentives. Share the cards at session's end and send bona fide local love with your holiday greetings.

Another idea: give the gift of a flower or veggie garden with plantable cards. Check out *www.greenfieldpaper.com and www.flower seedpaper.com* for beautifully designed cards with flowers and veggies inserted into recycled papers. Feeling super zealous? Check out *www.thriftyfun.com* for recipes on how to make your own plantable cards. Do some local crafting with your kids and send sustainable greetings. That's varsity local life Mom living!

If handiwork just won't work out, try *www.uncommongoods .com* for eclectic cards made from eco-friendly sources. Or visit *www.cardsforcauses.com* to find green cards that give back to good causes.

Sustainable Gifting

Sustainable gift-giving thrives with a mind-shift away from things and toward experiences. Jump-start your "experience gift" thinking with this section. When "something to do" still falls short of "something to have," as it may with kids, keep local and longevity principles top of mind. Still need something new and different? See the list of sustainable gifts later in this chapter for ideas on brand-new, but still green-themed gifts.

Wouldn't we all love a helping hand? Take a hint from your childhood "coupon book" days and give the gift of time. Carpooling, babysitting, grocery shopping, housecleaning, dog walking, massage giving—the list is as grand as your imagination.

Give the gift of karma: Do good on behalf of someone else. Pick a community cause and donate on behalf of your recipient or their children. Who wouldn't appreciate someone else greasing the path to good karma? Try *www.charitablenavigator.org* to find nonprofits serving your recipient's local community and pet cause.

Home delivery CSA style—the good local feasts: Augment culinary expertise, link the recipient to a local farmer, sneak greens into his or her diet, and save the planet! Sign someone up for a regular CSA delivery or buy a share in his or her local CSA (see Chapter 3 for CSA details).

Make 'em famous: Find a beloved locale and plant a tree in the name of a friend or family member. Or dedicate a neighborhood garden, highway mile, or beach cleanup to someone. Twinkle, twinkle, make your loved one a star—visit *www.starnamer.com* to name a star in your giftee's honor.

Carbon offsets: Celebrate someone's unique energy by softening his or her impact on Planet Earth. Guesstimate a carbon footprint and offset it with carbon credits (see Chapter 2 for details on how to do so). Or, fund an alternate energy source in someone's hometown under his or her name to offset home utility load.

Lighten their load (or at least their mail carrier's): Help your friends and family stop junk mail (and calls and e-mails) by signing them up for the "Do not mail," "Do not call," and "Do not e-mail" lists. You'll save their community reams of paper waste and save them time. Try services such as GreenDimes.com, StopTheJunkMail.com, and DoNotMail.org.

Save furry friends or their forest: Wouldn't your mother-in-law love to adopt a snow lion, or your nephew a meerkat? Check with their local zoo to see if you can sponsor an animal in someone's name. No zoo? Visit *www.worldwildlife.org* to make it real. Animals aren't your recipient's thing? How about promoting sustainability in an endangered arena and protecting a piece of the Amazon in his or her name? Check out *www.rainforest-alliance.org* to select your piece of wonderland.

Show your love with a talent show: Who wouldn't want to croon like you? Don't croon? Perhaps you paint, play piano, line dance, or simply deliver gut-busting comedy? Believe what your kindergarten teacher taught: we all have a talent. Share your Sudoku skills, knitting tips, or secret gooey brownie recipe demonstration with your friend. Speaking of which . . .

Cook it up: Show off your culinary gifts or fifth-generation beer bread recipe. Just make sure that what you make is really, really, really good (like something your kids would eat too) so you don't add to the food waste conundrum.

Girls' night out: Take the lead and schedule, plan, and attend a series of dates with your local ladies. Commit to an amount of time or number of events and put together a personal play series. Or plan the same kind of gift for your near and dear—we'd all love to shed the hassle around planning an event, date, or weekend away. Tell your beloved friends or family to simply show up. You do the rest.

Promote local learning: Give a membership, class series, or online subscription. Don't we all need a little more culture in our lives? (Or, at least some time at a zoo outside of our own homes?) Give a membership to the local children's museum, Gymboree class, art museum, yoga studio, or an online investing newsletter. Keep the main point in mind: *experience* beats *thing*.

Local Life Bundles: You've built a treasure trove of local recommendations and best of the best in your backyard. Why not package your expertise and encourage local living? Aggregate your favorite spots; create a local band mix CD; bundle gift certificates for local haunts; or offer Local Living 101 tutorials to jump-start your loved ones' local life learning.

Make your own gifts:

Music: My brother once gave me a three-disc compilation of his favorite music with pages detailing why he liked each song and what the music meant to him. So cool! Take the burned CD a bit further by telling a story about the music and why it matters to you and the recipient.

Write stuff: It takes time. It takes guts. And, it takes a few sheets of recycled paper. Write a story, poem, or ode to your loved one. Who cares about it being "good"? *You* are, and that's what matters.

Unleash your inner Martha: Paint a sunflower, knit a scarf, or tattoo your brand. Muster all your creative juices and let 'em rip on your beloved's behalf.

Digital photo album: Create an electronic photo book. Most web photo services offer a "make a book" tool. Make it and send the link instead of the paper.

"Brand New" Sustainable Gift Ideas

Still searching for the perfect gift? Many manufacturers and retailers are making "new" gift-giving hip, cool, and eco-friendly.

For Kids

For beautiful handmade toys, clothes, and gear, go to Nova Natural.com. Get lost on the website and emerge with "sustainable" and learning toys for your young ones. Go to ProgressiveKid.com to find a broad selection of sustainability-focused playthings sorted by age group. We love the Idbids starter kits, which include stuffed animals, interactive books, and charts to track eco-progress. Characters include icons for water, clouds, and flowers. The hand-pushed wooden animals (no batteries!) are always a hit. We needed a few at our home to keep kids peaceful at playdates.

YOU DON'T SEND ME FLOWERS (UNLESS THEY'RE LOCAL AND ORGANIC) ANYMORE . . .

As beautiful and cheerful as fresh flowers can be, they rate low on the sustainability scale. Fresh flowers certainly earn points as a reminder of our great outdoors, but they are a bit like Christmas trees: tough to justify against "reduce, reuse, and recycle" factors, and downright anti-local when conventionally harvested and shipped around the world.

When something fresh and green seems like the perfect gift or greeting, choose an "evergreen" option like an indoor plant or window herb garden. Better yet, donate to the Arbor Day Foundation and name a local tree after your beloved. If only, only, only fresh flowers will do the trick, shop online for local, organic flower options. They're pricier, but much better for the environment. You can check the shipping options to make sure your online provider sources its organic beauties from a grower near you.

To find the best fresh flowers and plant options, try *www.california organicflowers.com*, *www.organicbouquet.com*, or *www.Diamond organics.com* (grown in California and Hawaii). Also check the big sites such as 1800Flowers.com, ProFlowers.com, and FTD. They typically source from local providers and are expanding their organic offering regularly. To find organic growers near you, check out *www .LocalHarvest.org*. But remember, nothing beats bicycle-delivered flowers from the farmers' market.

When you're looking for the latest and greatest or want to check out the "sustainability screen" for certain gifts, visit Inhabitots.com. This site provides great kids' reviews for products in your local stores year-round.

Kate's Caring Gifts features a number of kids' DIY kits for things like chocolate and chewing gum. Since a tenet of local life and sustainability is a bias for doing things yourself, why not teach kids early, and make your job as a handy-crafty Mom relatively turnkey?

Shop EarthwiseKids.com to find a number of kid-friendly "get started" kits that teach how to save water, land, and nature. Come to think of it, they're not bad for grownups either.

For Him

If your sweetie likes to raise a pint every now and again, get to know your neighborhood hops haunts. Choose a local brew pub and sign up for a hands-on tasting tour as well as annual monthly delivery subscription. Toast your local life all year. If he likes to have a drink at home, try Benromach Organic Whiskey—it's richly delicious. Why not combine with a "coupon" for a night of "tasting" together too?

Honor the hero in your hero when you give good sustainability experiences in his name through Oxfam America Unwrapped. Plus, earn creativity and humor points by giving "a can of worms," a chance to "grow your own crocodile," or "fair trade honey" to your honey. Although these are global experiences, they do reinforce your local life guidelines by investing in local endeavors in a needy area.

Is your guy a nature or science buff? Try Planet Earth Five Disc DVD Series. The series makes the case for taking up the local life and sustainability cause. The collection is vast, striking, and (almost) as compelling as ESPN.

The Electrilite flashlight and cell phone charger—for the Maxwell Smart Bond man.

If your guy needs a radio for around the house or office, try the Magno Wooden Radio by Singgih Kartono. Kitsch, retro, and still cutting-edge, this hand-carved wooden radio will impress the music lover, the nature lover, or both.

For Her

Does any woman have enough candles? Freshen up her collection with soy, beeswax, and low-burn options from *www.illuminations.com* (search "soy") or *www.bigdipperwaxworks.com*.

Find hip and cool sustainable attire as well as signature bags (keep encouraging that no-disposable-bag behavior) for your favorite femmes at *www.HERDesign.com* and *www.Nau.com*.

For your jewelry-loving friends, give some bling from *www.BrilliantEarth.com*. The site sparkles with conflict-free goods and sustainability practices. Any piece would do.

For the indulgent indulgences, try organic lotions and potions. Try Therapy In A Box (Local and Fair Trade Kits), Pangea Gift Set, Clear Remedies Gifts, Blooming Lotus packages, and Saffron Rouge for more ideas.

Wrap Right

Oh so pretty for the recipient, but oh so ugly for your community, gift wrapping generates waste. Buck the trend and get creative in your wrap. Keep the three Rs top of mind: Reduce what you use; reuse any wrapping your receive; recycle what remains. Out of recycled wrapping materials? Flaunt it. Who says you have to hide your gift? Make the wrapping part of your gift. Tie the battery charger around the phone. Curl a scarf around the sweater. Make a purse to house the earrings. Knit a napkin to shroud the brownies. Or simply post a note on your gift saying you went naked and "skipped the wrap in the name of sustainability." You get the idea.

If you truly need a package, remember that the box counts. Check out the bags, paper, and cards made from "seed" paper. Simply plant the items in your own backyard, and up sprouts a garden. That's a gift that keeps on giving! Try *www.flowerseedpaper.com* or *www.botanicalpaperworks.com*.

What to do with those colorful leftover scraps of wrapping paper? Start a treasure trove box for arts and crafts (perhaps loot for next year's card craft day?). You can weave paper, create handmade books, or make handmade greetings with your kids.

And, remember: Don't throw your wrapping paper in the garbage or fireplace. It's often toxic and burns dirty.

Eat Local

The number one thing to do to improve your holiday feasts? *Eat less. Cook less. Buy less.* Avoid throwing away food by planning your meals with an eye to having one less serving than you need. If you still have leftovers, freeze them to improve the odds you'll eat full servings next go-around. Next best thing to buying less? Swap a meat dish for a veggie course. Once you've cleared those two hurdles, let the locavore shopping begin. Buy local, organic, fair trade, and free-range ingredients. Visit CSA websites (check out Chapter 3 for a list). Look for less packaging (think whole celery and onions instead of precut bagged). Honorable mentions? Avoid disposable serving items. If you can't do that, choose items made from recycled materials or bamboo. As always, recycle and reuse containers—even a one-time reuse of that French onion dip container is a good thing. Do it.

High-Impact Magic with Low Earth-Impact Décor

How to decorate with a sustainable heart? By now your local mantra is second nature. Remember your three Rs, steer clear of toxins (plastics), save power, and be kind to trees.

The Three Wise Rs

Save and reuse your décor as long as possible. When it's time for a fresh look, recycle your decorations locally through Craigslist or Freecycle. If they're beyond sharing (and even donating), recycle appropriately—use *http://earth911.com* to confirm how and where.

> → **Mom to Mom:** ←
> **Décor Swap Meet** 🏷️
>
> Instead of yet another white elephant party or cookie recipe exchange, set up a décor swap night with your girlfriends. Bundle up softly used decorative magic, bring a bottle of local wine, and voila! a new season of cheer awaits. Organize the swap early in the season, preferably in September to cover Halloween through New Year's (bonus points for Valentine's Day). Your home gets a facelift, your wallet gets a break, and your planet gets some relief. Trifecta!

Sustainable Pizzazz

You don't want toxins in your body or on your skin—why have them in ornaments or holiday décor? Evict toxins from your home tour. Shed plastics (especially PVC!), lead-laden painted pieces, and nonrecyclable items from interior design. Opt for handmade work, paper, wood, and even food-based materials. Fill containers (such as one of the umpteen glass floral vases crowding your kitchen cupboard) that you already have with seasonal treats. Recycle gift boxes into ornaments and door décor. Revert to childhood days and string popcorn or pasta with your block-party families. Starting from scratch? Set out to select products with small, soft earth-footprints: recyclable, biodegradable, fair trade, and lead-free.

Save Power

Light up celebrations with LEDs. They use less electricity and sparkle with more safety. Try *www.holidayleds.com* or *www.forever leds.com* for endless varieties. If you need to recycle lights, Holiday LEDs will do it for you. Send in your lights and get a coupon for 15 percent off LED lights in exchange. That's the holiday spirit! Or check out solar powered holiday lights at *www.gardeners.com*—an excellent solution for outdoor lighting creations.

Specific Holidays

Peruse the following for a few quick tips specific to annual celebrations as they unfurl on your calendar.

Birthdays

Keep thinking with your sustainability party hat on as you plan birthdays. Use digital invitations. Plan an outdoor day. Try earth-themed birthdays like local dirt digs (see birthday celebration options), neighborhood trail-hike treasure hunts, and community beach cleanup competitions. Stage a visit to the local nature conservatory instead of the pizza parlor, play games with eco-themes (pin the tail on the polar bear perhaps?), and serve locavore food. If you bring in outside talent (firefighters, face painters, or faux train conductors) encourage them to address the environment and sustainability in their relative context. And, although it may meet with lukewarm response as your kids grow up, consider passing on gifts and instead making donations in your birthday babe's name to a local sustainability cause.

Remember: Say no to non-renewable disposable serving items, décor, and balloons—a big no-no, much to most kids' dismay.

New Year's Day (January)

A gimme: New Leaf New Year's Resolutions await. You're already there with your Family Sustainability Plan! Bonus: provide an earth-friendly hangover helper—sweat, hair of the dog, or Bach Flower Remedies (an high-energy herbal substance mixed with thirty-eight flower essences and water) *www.bachflower.com*, recommended by the good-life thought leaders at TreeHugger.com.

Valentine's Day (February)

I know I hear a collective "ugh" out there. Valentine's Day is such a tricky holiday. As soon as the November/December holiday rush ends, we're supposed to gear up again to reprove our love for family and friends. Fight the urge to skip it and instead show off your love for Mama Earth as well as your family and beloved by hand-making gifts. Make your Valentines from recycled (almost) anything. Stand out with kitschy heart-shaped greetings made from old CD covers or pages torn out of a favorite book, with best passages highlighted. Get creative with heart-shaped veggie cutouts and cookie treats. And, skip the fresh flowers unless they are CSA or farmer's-market specials—the markup alone is unlovable, and the often-unsustainable growing practices used to produce florists' flowers make Mama Earth's heart . . . blue.

Easter (April)

Be a good egg: stock up on free-range, local, organic eggs and plastic-free baskets (especially no plastic grass!) for Mrs. Easter Bunny. Make your own toxin-free egg décor. Boil water, vinegar, and "coloring" such as tea leaves (green, raspberry, blueberry), coffee grounds, or juices (cranberry, raspberry, lemonade) to create egg dye. Use soy crayons to color the eggs or wrap uncolored eggs in string to create patterns as you dye them.

Earth Day and Arbor Day (April)

What's not to love about celebrating Mama Earth? Make that Mama happy: go out into your community for some playtime, and clean up after yourselves when you're done. Organize a neighborhood trail or beach cleanup, plant a tree, or visit a neighborhood CSA. Take over the recycling for a local school or church that week, or tour a local landfill or recycling center.

BBQ Holidays (Memorial Day, July 4, and Labor Day)

Though BBQs are tough to make truly sustainable, at least you're enjoying the great outdoors. Best things to do to orient your 'Q to the earth's longevity: Eat more veggies (local) and less meat. Burn clean: lump coal beats briquettes (which release coal dust); electric and propane beat charcoal; and solar powered beats them all. Check out Home Depot and Lowe's for reasonably priced options. For a crowd-pleasing high-tech gadget, consider the Tammock Solar Powered Grill. Use a chimney starter instead of lighter fluid (high VOC). For somewhat sustainable supplies, try Char-Broil.com. Rainforest Alliance Smartwood certified their products.

Back to School (September)

Purge the house, donate and recycle excess, restock critical provisions with recycled gear for new school needs, and choose green school supplies. Try *www.inhabitat.com* for a broad selection of everything from pens and binders to signature notebooks and lunch containers.

Halloween (October)

What a holiday to show off your local prowess! Dress up, feast, and decorate with shades sustainable, local living. Keep the following ideas top of mind.

Bring back dress-up time: Did anyone else dress up in their mom's clothes every year until high school? What happened to making costumes from the contents of home closets? Go retro and earn creativity points: dress up in something from home, make your own costume, or shop vintage boutiques. If you have to buy your get-up, stay far, far away from plastic. Again, PVC is truly scary. Bygone, outgrown costumes or components? Recycle or swap with other moms. Our local parent's club does a Halloween costume swap. On the designated Saturday in September, families bring in truly gently used costumes to exchange for "tickets." On Sunday, families return to trade in each ticket for a "new" costume. It's a great reuse event and a fun way to show your kiddos how to shop for great recycled goods. To find eco-friendly face paint and hair products as well as a whole host of ghoulish ideas, try *www.greenhalloween.org.*

Sustainable sweet treats: Shop local, organic sources for your pumpkins and chocolates. At the risk of earning the "Grinch-ess Who Stole Halloween" title, consider skipping candies all together. Most data tells us that as a nation, we could stand to lose candy-caused pounds around our waists as well as candy-wrapper waste in our landfills. Alternative bag "treat" drops include nuts, crackers, or scary stickers. Try *www.localharvest.org* to find nearby pumpkin crops.

Reverse trick-or-treat: Global Exchange offers a way to give back while indulging chocolate decadence. Hooray! Sign up on *www.global exchange.org* to get free samples of Fair Trade chocolates as well as cards detailing the fair trade certification program. You and your kids hand out the chocolates and the cards as you trick-or-treat door-to-door to heighten appreciation of cocoa farmers and their challenges. A nice surprise for neighbors, extra chocolates for all, and increased awareness about the benefits of supporting Fair Trade businesses.

Use reusable goody bags: Earn the treats and skip the tricks by carrying a reusable goody bag. Or, remember a tried and true "reuse" strategy: pillowcases. Just remember to watch out for what's hidden under your kids' pillows come November . . .

Decorate green: Lose the petroleum and light up Mr. Jack's Lantern with sustainable-resource candles such as soybean or beeswax. Or swap one-time-use candles for reusable LED lights.

Recycling Day (November 15)

At last—a holiday your local living family can embrace for its true-blue sustainability intentions! Celebrate The Big "R" by organizing a neighborhood recycling drive, picking up trash and recyclables on local trails, and purging your home of bigger recyclables such as clothes, electronics, and furniture. If your children's schools don't yet celebrate the day, add it to the school calendar and raise recycling awareness in classrooms. To learn more, visit *www.nrc-recycle.org.*

Thanksgiving (November)—A Locavore's Paradise

Yum. A holiday to satiate the food-o-phile in us all. Keep Thanksgiving grounded in its namesake by treading lightly on our planet. Choose local, organic menu items. Cut back a bit on the turkey (and any other meats) in exchange for a few more (seasonal) greens. Dial back the portions and then rev up the composting. At a minimum, separate the beets your son hid in his napkin from the turkey your grandmother skipped. Doing so gets the green food waste in your green-waste trash can and the non-green waste (meats, bones, and extremely soiled napkins) into the other trash can. Of course, your recycle bin will be overloaded with bottles and cans, right?

For a cheat sheet of what might be in season in your community during Thanksgiving, scan the following:

Root vegetables: carrots, potatoes, sweet potatoes, and yams
Other vegetables: artichoke, asparagus, beets, broccoli, cabbage, cauliflower, leek, mushrooms, spinach
Fruits: banana, lemon, orange
Honey (and beeswax for candles)

For the main event, choose an organic, free-range, antibiotic-free turkey. Try OrganicPrairie.com or Mary's Turkeys *www.marys turkeys.com* for tasty birds.

Stay basic for your décor with cornstalks, gourds, pumpkins, or a full-blown cornucopia. See *www.RealSimple.com* and *www.Kids Crafts.com* to learn how to make one yourself. *Remember: When you cook, use your microwave as much as you can, then the toaster oven, then the stovetop, and the oven as a last choice.*

Christmas / Chanukah (December)

These are the mothers of all holiday celebrations: Christmas and Chanukah! In addition to all of the Local Life Guidelines, December brings questions of eco-friendly Christmas trees and menorahs. For menorahs, consider those made of recycled materials lit with soy-based candles. Trees present a trickier conundrum. "Real" trees often mean forest waste, toxic agriculture, and large, eco-footprint trucking. "Fake" trees equal plastic and most of the time—yikes!—PVC. For many, skipping a tree conjures up Grinch-esque sentiments. Good-living locavores often advise buying a tree such as a ficus, palm, or even bonsai tree to then replant after Christmas. However, planting may outstretch your skill set, dwelling size, or land rights. What to do? If you must have a tree (and our family does), buy a real one from a local, organic, sustainable forest source. To find such a source, start with your local CSA, co-op, or Whole Foods. To find an organic tree farm near year, check out *www.greenpromise.com*. Don't forget to treat the tree as you would other green recyclables. Many local recycling services do a special tree pick up the first two weeks post the Christmas holiday. If your locale does not, investigate a chipping service, which could create mulch from your celebratory tree.

TRA LA LA LA

For one of the warmest, coziest get-to-know-your-neighbors events, bring back door-to-door caroling. Our meal co-op leader, Kristin K., also organizes an annual holiday caroling tour. She invites a homeful of neighbors, serves CSA-sourced yums-yums and quenchers, provides a living room pre-caroling practice session, and then leads the march around the 'hood. As we stroll door to door with warm wassail, we visit friends, learn about new additions (one year's highlight was three-week-old Pressley T. greeting carolers) and put names to dog-walking friends' faces. Bundle up and bask in the neighborly cheer.

"Stop worrying about the potholes in the road and celebrate the journey!"
—Barbara Hoffman

13

YOUR BEST FRIEND: BACKYARD, SUSTAINABLE PET CARE

> "Animals are such agreeable friends—they ask
> no questions, they pass no criticisms."
>
> —George Eliot

Of all family members, our furry friends probably live the closest to the patch of the earth we're hoping to save. Set up your pet's life to be sustainable by stocking locavore fuel and toys, mindfully cleaning up their waste, and keeping your home in its natural earth-loving state. If you're just getting ready to add a pet to your home life, start off on the right path by shopping a shelter first.

EYE OPENERS
- During an average cat's life, a pet owner throws out close to 2,000 pounds of cat litter.
- Eighty percent of pet owners celebrate pets' birthdays and holidays via gift-giving.
- The average dog eats—and then excretes—twenty-six pounds of preservatives a year.

THE LOCAL LIFE GUIDELINES: YOUR PETS

1. Shelter a sheltered friend.
2. *Food:* Choose organic, local, and homemade.
3. *Cleanup care:* Composting saves the day.
4. *Toys:* Search for local life playthings.
5. Make your home sustainable for your pet friends, too.

The Sustainability Screen: Your Pet

Change the World

IMPACT

Baby Steps Count

1. Start Here!

Choose local, organic food products

Look for a higher percentage of "meal" versus "meat" in foods

Choose organic grooming products

Use biodegradable bags for cleanup

Use filtered water for pets

3. Reach For It!

Find your family friend from a shelter

Compost pet waste

Survey your home for pet-friendly practices: pass on nonstick pans, stain-proofing, and insecticides

2. Why Not?

Make a bed for your pet from organic materials

Choose vegetarian food products

Stock sustainability-oriented pet toys

Switch to biodegradable litter

Keep cats as indoors-only pets

4. Save for Last!

Make your own pet food

Simple　　　　　　　　**EASE TO DO**　　　　　　　　Disruptive

The Nitty Gritty: Your Pets

You can love your family's furry friend while loving the earth. Earth-friendly pet food and gear can be found at your local pet shop. Sustainable cleanup options are pretty easy to put in place. And, finding your pet in an earth-friendly place, such as a shelter, starts you off with Mama Earth's interests at heart.

Shelter a Sheltered Friend

After acquiescing to the wide-eyed, oh-so-heart-melting "Mom, can we puhlleeezzzeee have a [dog, cat, gerbil, whatever]??!!!?" plea, consider the pet's source. As you add to your fold, check out a shelter first. Although 20 million four-legged babes arrive each year, sadly, we euthanize close to four million. With less than 10 percent of pet owners finding furry friends at shelters, imagine the sustainability impact we'd have by giving sheltered pets a home. Most shelters make sure their animals are spayed/neutered and housebroken, which makes transition into your home neat and easy. And, since shelters usually require a family "interview" and approval process, you can feel good that the shelter's working hard to match the right pet to your home. Try *www.adoptapet.com* or *www.petfinder.com* to find a shelter and/or a sheltered pet near you.

If you can't find the one you love at a shelter, consider your local shelter for family volunteer efforts. Many hold pet parades and volunteer days where your kids—and pets—can donate time to help homeless animals. The work that shelters do to care for and place abandoned animals cleans our collective conscience as well as Mama Earth.

Unless you want to feed, shelter, and raise many (many) small ones for a lifetime, remember to neuter or spay your pet. We already have more pets than we need. Plus, spaying and neutering can be good for your pet's health. Doing so helps stave off a myriad of possible prostate, ovarian, testicular, and uterine diseases.

THE LAST TUESDAY IN FEBRUARY — NATIONAL *WHAT* DAY?

Yes, there is indeed a National Spay Day. Preventing unwanted animal births is important not only to protect your community from the implicit residual waste, but also to ensure that more animals end up in pleasant places such as warm homes instead of desolate places such as cold alleys. So, celebrate National Spay Day by either spaying/neutering a newcomer to your home (many local organizations reimburse you for the cost that day) or participating in fundraising events for your local shelter. Mark your calendar in ink: National Spay Day—the last Tuesday in February.

Finally, remember that as soon as you choose your pet, you should get him tagged with an ID chip. You may be surprised at what an escape artist your new family member is (or at how often the gate's left open by your bigger babies). Most vets will insert the electronic chip with your contact information so Good Samaritans can help your pet find his way home. Lost your pet? Try *www.pet911.com.*

Food: Local, Homemade, and Organic

A couple of thoughts to bear in mind when selecting your pet's feast: what goes into your pet, comes out of your pet—literally—into your backyard. And, crazy as it sounds, whatever pet food doesn't end up in our pets' bellies often ends up as feed to animals sold for *our* bellies. That's right: unsold pet food often feeds chickens or pigs. So, even if you don't have a pet or not everyone in your family engages in pet cuisine concern, everyone could stand a little Pet Food 101. Pet food need not meet gourmet hurdles, but some basic guidelines make sense for sustainability. Ingredient label vigilance matters.

Note: In 2007, contaminated pet food drove the largest product recall in consumer history.

As you do with people chow, choose local, organic, and free-range pet feasts. Certified organic pet products must meet USDA standards including no hormones, artificial preservatives, pesticides, or artificial or genetically engineered ingredients. When you can't go local or organic, say no to the following:

"By-products": This moniker does not mesh with sustainability. It often means animal parts and waste not meeting "meat" guidelines. This set of "by-products" can include diseased organs and other "waste" materials that would otherwise have to be thrown away. Many times these items are known as "4-D," which stands for "Dead, Dying, Diseased, or Down (Disabled)" while at the slaughterhouse. No, no, no, no good.

"Meat" versus "Meal": "Meal" contains a higher percentage of protein (instead of water and grain) than do "meat" ingredients. More protein equals better fuel for your friend. So, although it may seem counterintuitive, look for foods with "meal" listed earlier in the ingredients label. Because FDA labeling requires panels to list ingredients from highest to lowest percentage, what you find first on the panel you'll find most in the product (this goes for people food too).

BHA, BHT, and ethoxyquin: These ingredients are used as preservatives to extend shelf life. However, these additives can cause liver and kidney damage as well as skin reactions, dental disease, and allergies. Ethoxyquin, which is regulated as a pesticide, is a possible carcinogen. The FDA allows tiny amounts of it in human food, but high amounts in pet food. You may see it listed as "E" in the ingredient panel.

Fish poisons: Since cat food often contains fish parts, you'll want to switch up your kitty's meals to vary her exposure to fish toxins (such as mercury).

Try Canidae/Felidae Pet Foods (*www.canidae.com*), Country Pet Frozen Pet Foods (*www.countrypet.com*), Natura Pet Products (*www.naturapet.com*), and Newman's Own (*www.newmansown .com*). ⬛ PetCo and PetSmart offer organic food and pet care at reasonable prices. They also offer regular coupons to help offset the 15–20 percent premium for organic eats. And finally, when quenching your friend's thirst, think about using filtered water. A sink or pitcher filter does the trick.

Cleanup and Care

Perhaps the toughest thing about life with our fine furry friends? Their waste—okay, poops. Most pet poop ends up in community landfills sealed for eternity in those pesky nonbiodegradable bags. Or worse, a bad karma pet parent leaves waste on the grass or sidewalk to wash into our waterways. Boo.

Need I suggest that "poop scooping" falls high on the kids' chore list? When your children attack the pet cleanup, a few rules of thumb help. First, use biodegradable bags. Check out *www.pawshop.com/ scbipopimiba.html* for options. Considering the compost conundrum? You can compost poop, but don't use it in your veggie patch. Pet poop can contain things like *E. coli*. Want to go high-tech for your dog poop? Check out the Doggie Dooley—a "dog toilet" that uses enzymes to reduce waste to a liquid that's absorbed into the ground. See *www.doggiedooley.com* for more.

Kitty Non-Litter

Conventional cat litter comes from a clay, sodium bentonite, which sheds carcinogenic silicon particles as your cat scratches or you poop-scoop postmess. Hooray for better—biodegradable—options: recycled newspaper or magazines, and plant-based litters (corn, grass, wheat, pine, or cedar). Remember: Never flush cat litter. Cat feces can contain parasites that are no-no's for waterways and ocean life.

Pets still potty training? Hand your kids your all-natural cleaners like vinegar, lemon, and baking soda to clean up. Two great litters to try: Swheat Scoop—so natural that TreeHugger claims it can even be eaten without issue (well, probably some taste issues, but stomachs should be A-Okay) and World's Best Cat Litter. Find them at PETCO or *www.PetFoodDirect.com*.

Pet Glamour

Choose nontoxic pet personal care to make kitty, pup, bunny (and so on) shine. Check the labels for ingredients as you would in your products. Biggest offender reminders: no parabens, artificial color or fragrances, PEG, urea, phosphates, sulfites, or ingredients that have "eth" in their names. You can use the Environmental Working Group (EWG) personal care database for humans to check out pet products (*www.cosmeticsdatabase.com*). No label? No purchase. No way.

TO FLEA OR NOT TO FLEA (COLLAR)?

The sustainability-oriented pet community debates the efficacy and toxicity of flea collars. Flea collar products are still labeled as "safe," but the long-term effects of their strong ingredients are yet unknown. As an alternative approach to flea management, try frequent pet baths, home vacuuming, and less-toxic treatments such as herbals (pennyroyal) or feeding your pet garlic and yeast (provides extra Vitamin B and makes your pets less palatable to fleas). The daily dose for dogs is a few garlic cloves (a little less for smaller four legged friends and little more for the bigger ones) and a quarter cup of yeast; for cats, one clove of garlic and a teaspoon of yeast. But beware—too much garlic (or onions) can cause anemia in dogs. Check with your vet for details.

To find fine pet finesse, sample the glamour gear below. Shop *www.cybercanine.com*, *www.amazon.com*, *www.ecopetlife.com*, or *www.petstore.com* for:

- Mundo Canine Products
- Buddy Wash
- Eco-Me Cat and Dog starter grooming kits
- Spike Products

Feel-Good Playthings

Help Fido frolic with local and earth-loving toys. Recycle old clothes, socks, and rope into homemade toys. Stay toxin-free by choosing sustainable materials such as hemp and organic cottons. Avoid all gear made from PVC-laden plastics. If you need to buy pet toys, try the ones made by West Paw (*www.westpawdesign.com*), Eco-Pet (*www.ecopetla.com*), and Natural Pet Mart (*www.naturalpetmart.com*) also carry a good line of hemp as well organic cotton playthings. When your pet's ready to rest, deliver him to sweet dreams in a bed made from organic cotton. Check out *www.anniessweatshop.com*; she'll make your pet's bed out of one of your old pillows. Smelling like you, it will comfort your pet while it adds to your family reuse scorecard.

IN HERE, KITTY, KITTY . . .

Did you know that housecats are the leading killer of birds? Yup, more than a million birds die each year in the grips of our beloved kitties. Most vets recommend that cats play indoors. It turns out the great outdoors is not so great for domestic cats or for your neighborhood life. Thanks to cars, disease, and predators, the average lifespan of an outdoor/indoor cat is less than three years, while an indoors-only cat can make it to fifteen years. Consider an enclosed outdoor play space if your cat must have fresh air.

Make Your Home Sustainable for Your Friends

Chances are your family sustainability efforts have made your home uber–pet friendly too. Consider a few watch-outs for the most pet-friendly home. Skip the nonstick pans. Overheating in nonstick pans can release toxic gases. Even small doses threaten smaller pets such as birds or hamsters. Pass as well on stain-proofing furniture. Many stain-resistant treatments ooze toxic perflurochemicals (no good for us or our four-legged friends). Instead, opt for baking soda pastes for any "incident" cleanups. Avoid conventional lawn insecticides. Many insecticides do their dirty work via carcinogenic chemicals that can cause organ and nervous system damage. Last, remember to count your pet in your family carbon offsets—their consumption and wastes add up even after your green scrubbing efforts. Hungry for more eco-friendly pet-care tips? Visit *www.pets fortheenvironment.org* and *www.greatgreenpet.com* for Eco Pet Life 201 and 301.

Spotlight: The Atlanta Humane Society

According to the ASPCA, between 8 million and 12 million animals enter a shelter each year. Most shelters are split fifty-fifty between cats and dogs and receive animals evenly from pet owners and animal control. In addition to caring for animals and working to find them homes, shelters offer a broad range of services, from grooming and veterinary care to ID-chipping pets and providing pet therapy to hospitals and nursing homes. Sadly, due to animal overpopulation, shelters also must manage euthanization programs for almost half the animals they receive.

See the advice below from Schuyler Rideout, marketing manager for the Atlanta Humane Society, on how to best support your local shelter as well as tips for finding your next furry friend.

How can people get involved with their local shelter?

Every local shelter runs a calendar full of events and fundraisers where families can volunteer with hands-on help or through contributions. Even in the absence of a shelter fundraiser, your family can help raise money to donate by organizing a bake sale or collecting recyclables to exchange for cash. Families also can donate newspapers, grocery bags, and towels for the local shelter to use.

How should someone who wants to adopt a pet go about it?

Every shelter differs, but most require an adoption interview and qualification process to help ensure that pets end up in a healthy home. Families should allow an hour or so at a minimum to talk with an adoption counselor and meet potential pets in order to choose their animal. Feel good knowing that in effect, "recycling" a shelter pet is saving a life.

To find a shelter near you, try *www.pets911.com*, *www.world animal.net*, *www.adoptapet.com*, *www.petfinder.com*, or *www.hsus.org* for the Humane Society office near you.

> "The greatness of a nation and its moral progress can be judged by the way its animals are treated."
> —Mahatma Gandhi

14

SUSTAINING THE FUN: MEDIA AND ENTERTAINMENT

> "They talk of the dignity of work. Bosh. The dignity is in leisure."
>
> —Herman Melville

Local life extends—and excels—at play time as well. Thanks to the Internet, recycling tired media can be easy and, if the items have been well loved, profitable. As you select new media, search your community talent and discover musicians, celebs, and writers earning kudos for their local life and sustainability-oriented work.

A number of gadgets can aid in your family's local living efforts. Consider sustainability winners such as solar powered media players and electronic book readers to continue small steps to better living.

EYE OPENERS

- A big-screen TV used for just half the waking day generates half a ton of greenhouse gases (GHG) per year. (Remember: the average amount of "controllable" GHG emissions per person per year is ten tons.)
- You can power a laptop for an hour with the amount of energy it takes to make just four sheets of paper.

The Sustainability Screen:
Your Media and Entertainment

Change
the World

1. Start Here!

Reduce screen time—get outside

Recycle media

Legally download content instead
of buying physical copies

Add to your collection via reused
and swap sources

Add local-life books to your family
reading list

Save power with consoles: power
down or off when not in use

3. Reach For It!

Consider upgrading consoles to
power-saving models

Consider choosing the more
efficient Nintendo Wii if adding
new game consoles

Try a digital book reader

Buy products made from recycled
media

Use alternate energy chargers for
media players

IMPACT

2. Why Not?

Organize a media swap with
friends and neighbors

Support local musicians, authors,
and celebs

Add sustainability-oriented video
games, CDs, and DVDs to the
family library

Use at-the-source power strips
for media

4. Save for Last!

Recycle old media into
handmade gifts

Add your own earth-friendly
outdoor playground

Unplug

Baby Steps
Count

Simple   **EASE TO DO**   Disruptive

LOCAL LIFE GUIDELINES: MEDIA AND ENTERTAINMENT

1. *Reduce, reuse, recycle at play:* CDs, DVDs, video games, and books.
2. *Support local talent:* Musicians, celebs, and writers.
3. *Choose sustainable gear:* Media players, consoles, and digital readers.
4. *Play:* Throughout the neighborhood on earth-friendly play sets.

WHAT ABOUT NON-ELECTRONIC— SUSTAINABLE—INDOOR TOYS?

Since so many toys have been found to carry toxins such as lead, phthalates, and PVC, screen "reused" toys and select only those not made of plastic, painted wood, or metal. Also, stay away from new plastics. Unfortunately the cheaper the toy, the more likely it is to have higher toxin levels. Opt for wood and organic-fiber toys when you can.

Consider some of the up-and-coming manufacturers of handmade toys—especially treasures made in your locale. Not only are the toys sustainable and toxin-free, they also expose children to the beauty and ingenuity of quality craftsmanship. If you can't find a local artisan, feel good trying Faggo. We've loved Faggo handmade wooden rolling toys. The line includes trucks, utility vehicles, bulldozers, RVs, and boats. They're made in Germany by handicapped artisans.

The Nitty Gritty: Media and Entertainment

Before diving in to screen-time guidelines, flip back to Chapter 9 for more outdoor play ideas and inspiration. Outdoor play uses your own energy, requires only limited gear, and reacquaints you with the local community you're saving. It is much easier to have "family time" together when you're playing outside, rather than sitting in front of individual screens indoors. It's also easier to get to know your community of neighbors, businesses, and secret treasures when you spend time out and about your town. And, it's virtually impossible to help kids (and grownups) appreciate, never mind yearn for, a better community and local life when they find most of their recreation burrowed inside, away from it. Consider swapping an hour a week from media to sunshine and celebrate a local life victory.

Reduce, Reuse, Recycle at Play— CDs, DVDs, Video Games, and Books

When your family does plug in, keep local and sustainability fundamentals in mind to limit your media's earth footprint.

Reduce: Legally download content

Bypass sticky copyright issues by starting with a commitment to *legally* download as much media as possible. Yes, disk space and computing power consume energy, but the reduction in manufactured plastic, paper, and processed metals pays off. See the Sustainable Gear list in this chapter for ideas on sustainable media players and digital readers. Sites to try for downloads:

Pandora—create and stream radio channels customized to your favorite musical flavor.

iTunes.com—has most mass-market music and broad independent selection as well.

EMusic.com—offers more than 4.5 million tracks with an emphasis on indie labels. Some tracks are priced at twenty-five cents.

Allmusic.com—on the web since 1995, All Music offers detailed profiles, comparisons, and reviews so you can research genres and artists. You can listen as well as watch artist videos to narrow your purchases.

Wolfgangsvault.com—live concerts from Bill Graham's vaults. You'll be surprised at what you find; almost fifty musicians including Aerosmith, Bo Diddley, Tom Petty, Little Feat, Springsteen, and U2. Many concerts are free to download.

Lala.com—put your CD library online and trade with others. You send in your CDs, and Lala digitizes them for resale. If you don't have one they need, it will cost ten cents to seventy-nine cents per song (depending on whether it's web access only or MP3 download) to buy what you'd like.

Reuse and Recycle Your Play

Still need a physical copy of family's favorite songs and shows? A veritable subculture of stores carrying music, games, and books exists to support your sustainability efforts. Here are some of the best places for amping up your family's collections.

For all media, online standbys like Craigslist, Freecycle, and eBay are good options. SwitchPlanet.com is dedicated just to CDs, DVDs, video games, and books.

For music and movies, good online options include EcoEncore. org, Half.com (owned by eBay), Secondspin.com, SwapaCD.com (swap for free), Spun.com, TheCDexchange.com, or Zunafish.com. For rare finds try *www.musicstack.com*. If discs in your collection are too damaged to trade, try *www.greendisk.com* to recycle them.

For video games, the chain stores GameStop, PlayNtrade, and HMV offer trade-in programs that allow you to earn discounts by bringing in old games and consoles. Online, try *www.goozex.com*, *www.recycle-video-games.com*, and *www.rvgnet.net*. Of course, renting games via Blockbuster, Netflix, or your local library earns green points as well.

In addition to Amazon, try Half Price Books to buy and sell used books, both online (*www.halfpricebooks.com*) and at store locations. For a great free option, check out PaperbackSwap.com. Find what you like, and find someone to swap with.

LOVE YOUR MEDIA TO MAKE THEM LAST

It's tough to recycle or swap your treasures if they're too worn down to share. Take the best care of your content by keeping CDs, DVDs, and videos covered and out of the sun, heat, and water. Too late to do so? You can still salvage worn discs. Fix small scratches by rubbing toothpaste in a circle from the center to the edges. For books, practice your memory skills and note the page you nodded off on in your mind's eye instead of dog-earing the page. A little TLC eases reduce-and-reuse efforts.

Note: Make tossing media in the recycling bin a last resort. Donate whatever remains postswap to the local library, church, school, Salvation Army, or Goodwill. Although most media can be converted and reused by recycling, it does take energy to do so. And, of course, landfills are never aficionados of quality music, movies, and literature.

Bonus: *Reinforce*

When it's time to add "new" new content, choose media made from recycled materials with less packaging and carbon-neutral manufacturing. Many CDs and DVDs publicize or highlight that they are made of eco-materials and reduced packaging. In order to simplify your selections, the next section includes a short list of musicians and celebs earning green stars specifically for their eco-production efforts.

Support Local Talent—Musicians, Celebs, Writers

Dig into your local scene and support musicians, writers, and other creatives hard at work next door. Fuel their efforts by buying their work. The Internet has made identifying, researching, and sampling local music more than accessible. Get started with the websites listed here and then create locavore expertise in the creative arts. Bonus points for artisans focusing on a sustainable bent in their creations.

Surf sites for a sampling of your local music scene and then craft your musical tour. Enlist your family and friends to sort the scene for top weekly shows. If you structure a family calendar, feature picks from everyone and embark on your own magical mystical ride. To begin, sample *www.projectopus.com*, *www.localmusicguide.net*, and *www.localmusicdirectory.com*. If you haven't found anything promising, a Google search for "local music scene" will bring up a long list of music by towns.

Mind-shift from mass destruction to mass preservation with green video games. The games featured here earn rave reviews for both eco-focus and good game play. To find more, visit *www.getgamesmart.com*, *www.kidsites.com*, *www.edutainingkids.com*, and *www.gamingwithchildren.com* for kid-friendly reviews.

For preschoolers, try *Go San Diego Go: Safari Rescue*. For your elementary-aged kids, try *The Big Green Help Global Challenge* (Nickelodeon) *Endless Ocean*, *Snapshot Adventures: Secret Bird Island*, and *Viva Piñata*.

For your kids in middle school and older, good choices include *Adventure Ecology*, *A New Beginning*, *Chibi-Robo: Park Patrol*, *Eco-Creatures: Save the Forest*, *Global Warning*, and *Second Life*, which converts virtual planted trees (for $1.50 per tree) into real trees through the Second Chance Tree organization. Also explore Starbucks' *Planet Green Game* at *www.planetgreengame.com* or try building a new virtual city according to eco-principles via the Sim City games and GreenCity.

> → **Mom to Mom:** ←
> **Swap Meets Media**
>
> Have faith that your neighbors and friends tire of movies, music, and games as quickly as your family does. Take advantage of short shelf lives to stock your entertainment shelves via neighborhood, church, school, or playgroup swaps. Set up a biannual swap to keep CDs, DVDs, games, and books fresh. You may have the best luck organizing this one through your school and/or church since you can aggregate content by age level. Remember to utilize common rating systems for quality and age-appropriateness. Use color-coded markers to "rate" items for quick swapping.

Seeding Local Life and Sustainability Screens with Kids

Take advantage of all the enthusiasm and passion that have come to earth-saving efforts throughout recent years and offer kids books slanted to local and sustainability efforts.

Ever ponder the messages your daily reading rituals impart? Of course you do. But sometimes even the most earnest moms get lost in reaching for the closest book to collapse into bed time routines. As magical as books like *Where The Wild Things Are* and *Good Night Moon* can be, sprinkle in some sustainability messaging with story telling magic. The books below offer a good dose of good citizenship packaged in an engaging tale. Peruse the age group lists for books appropriate for your young minds.

- Preschool
  - *The Berenstain Bears Don't Pollute Anymore*
  - *The Earth and I*
  - *On The Day You Were Born*
  - *Brown Bear, Brown Bear What Do You See*
  - *Michael Recycle*
  - *Whole World* (with a sing-along CD)

- Elementary School
  - The Dr. Seuss classic *Lorax*
  - *The Great Trash Bash*
  - *The Everything Kids' Environment Book*
  - *Where Does Garbage Go?*
  - *A Child's Introduction to the Environment*
  - *The Dirt on Dirt*
  - *It's Earth Day!*
  - *Skip Through the Seasons*
  - *The Boy Who Grew Flowers*

- Middle School and Older
  - *You Are Here* (great local and global anecdotes give compelling answers to a cynical "why bother?")
  - *Fifty Ways to Save the Ocean*
  - *It's Easy Being Green* (Sustainability 101)
  - *The Live Earth Global Warming Survival Handbook* (engaging scenarios and graphics)

To find more choices, try *www.ecochildsplay.com*. And, remember, the library offers one of the most tried-and-true local life options around.

Searching for more local media to entertain your family? Start with local and sustainability-oriented portals and search engines. Thanks to the Internet, ever-expanding product and resource lists await you. Start with *www.local.com* and *www.locallectual.com* to sift through community providers. Then visit standard sustainability-oriented portals such as MSN Green (*www.green.msn.com*), The Daily Green (*www.thedailygreen.com*), and Yahoo Green (*www .green.yahoo.com*). Take it an extra step with *www.Blackle.com*. Since a black screen uses less power than a white one, the Blackle search engine saves energy while you're searching.

Sustainable Gear—
Media Players, Consoles, and Digital Readers

Green your current gear by turning it off and unplugging it when not in use. When you're ready for new toys, look for power-saving features, wind or solar power sources, and rechargeable batteries. The following options have received good reviews.

Power Plus Player is a wind-up player. One minute of winding yields up to twenty minutes of playtime for your DVD, iPod, or other media players. In addition, the wind-up charger can power your cell phone. And, with wind-up players you at least get a little bit of physical exertion along with your screen time.

The eMotion Player is a solar powered music and video player. Shiro SQ-S, also solar powered, delivers thirty-five hours of music or seven hours of video for every four hours in direct sunlight.

Need to charge up? Freeloader, hYmini, and Solio offer weighty solar powered universal charger options.

Looking to add the ubiquitous video game console to your house? The Natural Resources Defense Council (NRDC) studied leading consoles and found the Nintendo Wii was seven to ten times more efficient than the Xbox or PlayStation.

You don't need to swap consoles to support sustainability. The NRDC estimates that 90 percent of console power usage can be reduced by powering off machines that aren't in play. Easy enough. Just encourage gaming companies to allow players to save point-in-play so your kids can pick up their games where they left off before dinner (and after homework).

Electronic readers have evolved over the past few years. If you (or more likely your kids) can stand smaller screens, most cell phones now have reader applications for book downloads. Apple's iPhone is particularly easy to read.

Larger-sized dedicated readers such as Amazon's Kindle and Sony's Reader now weigh less and simulate a real page format. Increased storage capacity means you can carry around two hundred books with you. Improved user interface design enables you to "dog ear" pages, make margin notes, and share excerpts. In addition to the Kindle and Reader, options include iRex iLiad, Franklin, and ectaco Jetbook. To find favorite books in e-versions, visit Ereader. com, Ebook.com, and Amazon.com.

Play Outdoors on Sustainable Play Sets

There are a few factors to be aware of when your kids are playing on public or personal play sets. Many contain tough chemicals such as chromium copper arsenate (CCA), which is used to treat wood; tremolite, a form of asbestos; and crystalline silica, a carcinogen sometimes found in play sand used in sandboxes.

If you have little ones and are looking to bring park play a little closer to home, try an earth-friendly play set. For home sets, look to buy gear made from Forest Stewardship Council (FSC) approved wood. Avoid CCA-treated woods, opting instead for naturally rot-resistant hardwoods like redwood or cedar or woods treated with ammoniacal copper quaternary (ACQ) or copper boron azole (CBA).

A more affordable play set may be made of rubber or metal. Look for those made from recycled materials and made with materials that can be recycled. To avoid tremolite and crystalline silica, buy sand designated as "made for play sets" versus commercial-grade sand.

Keep in mind a few TLC tips for the playground. Where possible, cover sandboxes tightly at night. A myriad of critters visit and can often leave undesirables behind. Treat a CCA-coated playground set as hazardous waste. Take care when breaking it down (use gloves and keep small children clear) and take it to your hazardous waste disposal location (reminder: check *www.911.org* to find your closest spot). If all of this information has left you feeling a bit zealous to learn about the quality of your local park's play set, test the wood and soil for arsenic with a kit from Environmental Working Group ($25; *www.ewg.org*).

SUSTAINABILITY-ORIENTED PLAY SET MANUFACTURERS

- CedarWorks (donates 10 percent of proceeds to children and eco-cause charities)
- Children's Play Structures
- Grounds for Play
- Kompan
- Play Mart

Pick up Oompa's eco-friendly play set to take to the sandbox ($9 at ToysRUs.com). *Remember: Always wash your kids' hands, and your own, postplayground.*

"He enjoys true leisure who has time to improve his soul's estate."

—Henry David Thoreau

RESOURCES

Books

Animal, Vegetable, Miracle: A Year of Food Life, by Barbara Kingsolver.

Gorgeously Green: 8 Simple Steps to an Earth-Friendly Life, by Sophie Uliano.

It's Easy Being Green: A Handbook for Earth-Friendly Living, by Crissy Trask.

The Lazy Environmentalist: Your Guide to Easy, Stylish, Green Living, by Josh Dorfman.

The Green Book: The Everyday Guide to Saving the Planet One Simple Step at a Time, by Elizabeth Rogers and Thomas M. Kostigen.

True Green: 100 Everyday Ways You Can Contribute to a Healthier Planet, by Kim McKay and Jenny Bonnin

You Are Here: Exposing the Vital Link Between What We Do and What That Does to Our Planet, by Thomas M. Kostigen.

Studies

Comparison of the Effects on the Environment of Polyethylene and Paper Carrier Bags (Federal Office of the Environment, August 1988).

Declining Fruit and Vegetable Nutrient Composition: What Is the Evidence? (Donald R. Davis, *Journal of HortScience,* February 2009).

Organic Industry Structure (Philip H. Howard, PhD, Michigan State University Study, July 2008: *www.msu.edu/~howardp*)

Websites
(✳ denotes favorite/primary source sites)

Hyper Locavore:
www.hyperlocavore.com

Local.com:
www.local.com

Local Lectual:
www.locallectual.com

Local.com:
www.local.com

Arbor Day Programs:
www.arborday.org

American Council for an Energy-Efficient Economy:
www.aceee.org

A Little Greener:
www.alittlegreener.com

AsureQuality Food and Agricultural Certification:
www.AsureQuality.com

Behind the Label:
www.behindthelabel.org

CCOF (Certified Organic Trade Association):
www.ccof.org

Center for Health, Environment and Justice:
www.chej.org

Climate Crisis:
www.climatecrisis.net

Climate Trust:
www.climatetrust.org

Close the Loop (recycled products portal):
www.closetheloop.com

Community Supported Agriculture Sources and Resources:
www.csacenter.org

Container Recycling Institute:
www.container-recycling.org

Cool Cities (Sierra Club):
www.coolcities.us

Cosmetics Database (SkinDeep):
www.cosmeticdatabase.com

Cradle to Cradle Certification:
www.c2ccertified.com

Daryl Hannah's dhlovelife:
www.dhlovelife.com

Database of State Incentives for Renewables and Efficiency:
www.dsireusa.org

Earth911 Recycling Resources:
http://earth911.com

The Eat Well Guide:
www.eatwellguide.org

Eco (The Place for Everything Eco):
www.eco.org

Eco Chick:
www.eco-chick.com

Eco Seek Search Engine:
www.ecoseek.net

Energy Information Administration:
www.eia.doe.gov

Energy Star:
www.EnergyStar.gov

Earth Day Network:
www.earthday.net

End Oil Initiative:
www.endoil.org

Fair Trade Federation:
www.fairtradefederation.org

Fair Trade USA:
www.TransFairUSA.org

Flex Your Power (California Energy Efficiency and Conservation):
www.fypower.com

Free from Plastic (Information and Product Recommendations):
http://freefromplastic.com

Food Alliance:
www.foodalliance.org

Forest Stewardship Council:
www.fscus.org

Global Organic Textile Standard:
www.global-standard.org

Great Green Goods Shopping Portal:
www.greatgreengoods.com

Green America (formerly Co-op America):
www.greenamericatoday.org

Green Biz (Business Voice of the Green Economy):
www.greenbiz.com

Green Cars:
www.greenercars.org

Green Certification: Green Seal:
www.greenseal.org

Green Earth Cleaning (dry cleaner resource):
www.greenearthcleaning.com

GreenHomeGuide:
www.greenhomeguide.com

Green Living Ideas:
www.greenlivingideas.com

Green Minded Wallet:
www.greenmindedwallet.com

Green Pages:
www.greenamericatoday.org/pubs/greenpages

Greenpeace:
www.greenpeace.org

Grist:
www.Grist.org

Green Guide:
www.thegreenguide.com

Hybrid Cars:
www.hybridcars.com

Ideal Bite:
www.IdealBite.com

Local Harvest (CSAs and Farmers' Markets):
www.localharvest.org

Local Pollution Scorecard:
www.scorecard.org

Low Impact Living:
www.lowimpactliving.com

Metro: People Places, Open Spaces (composting how-to's):
www.metro-region.org

N:Vision (lighting information):
www.nvisioncfl.com

National Geographic:
www.NationalGeographic.com

National Organic Standards Board (NOSB):
www.ams.usda.gov

National Resources Defense Council:
www.nrdc.org

Natural Food Network:
www.naturalfoodnet.com

The Nature Conservancy:
www.nature.org

New American Dream:
www.newdream.org

New Wind Energy:
www.newwindenergy.com

Old World Apothecary:
www.oldworldapothecary.com

Organic Consumers Association:
www.organicconsumers.org

Organic Exchange (Cotton Resource):
www.organicexchange.org

The Organic Make-Up Company:
www.theorganicmakeupcompany.com

The Organic Pages Online:
www.theorganicpages.com

Organic Spa Magazine:
www.organicspamagazine.com

Organic Trade Association:
www.ota.com

Parenting.com:
www.Parenting.com

Planet Green:
www.PlanetGreen.com

Plant a Tree USA:
www.plantatreeusa.com

Practical Environmentalist:
www.practicalenvironmentalist.com

Renewable Energy Sources:
www.green-e.org

The Road Less Traveled Resource Center:
www.roadlesstraveledstore.com

Safe Cosmetics:
www.safecosmetics.org

Safe (PVC-free) products:
www.besafenet.com

Save Our Environment:
www.saveourenvironment.org

Springwise:
www.springwise.com

SuperGreenMe:
www.SuperGreenMe.com

Sweathop Watch Group:
www.sweatfree.org

Thrifty Planet Resource Guide:
www.thriftyplanet.com

TreeHugger:
www.treehugger.com

True Food Network:
www.truefoodnow.org

U.S. Department of Energy: Energy Efficiency and
Renewable Energy:
www.eere.energy.gov

U.S. Department of Energy: Energy Savers:
www.energysavers.gov

U.S. Environmental Protection Agency:
www.EPA.gov

U.S. Green Building Council (LEED Certification):
www.usgbc.org

WaterSense:
www.epa.gov/watersense

Worldchanging:
www.worldchanging.com

Worldwatch Institute:
www.worldwatch.org

INDEX

About the Author

Linsly Donnelly is a businesswoman, yogini, and writer. In her most recent job of "Mom," Linsly awoke to the importance of investing in your community and leaving a viable earth behind for future generations. She is the cofounder of an e-commerce business and a yoga studio. A transplant from her beloved Texas, she savors splitting her time near the water (Dana Point) and in the mountains (Park City, Utah). Linsly fuels a few too many quests via a mocha addiction and the gleeful support of her valiant husband, their two high-energy children, and one very sleepy bulldog. She lives in Dana Point, California.